Haunting The Outer Banks

Joe Sledge

Other Books By Joe Sledge

Did You See That?
A GPS Guide to North Carolina's
Out of the Ordinary Attractions

Did You See That?
On The Outer Banks

Did You See That? Too!

Did You See That Ghost?

Haunting The Outer Banks

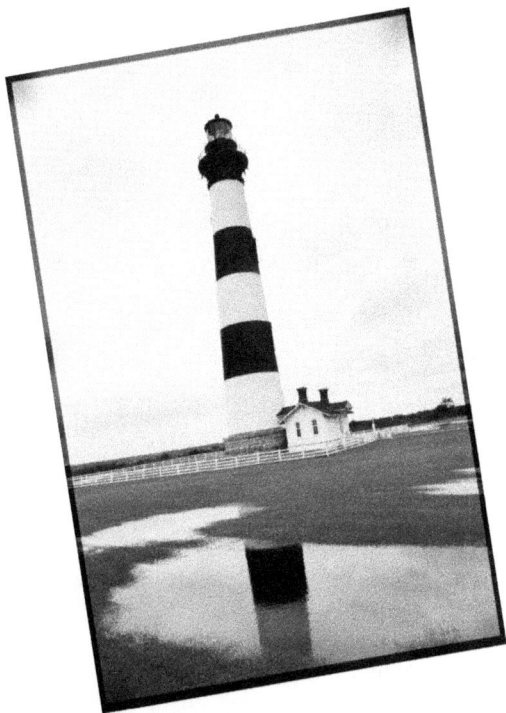

Thirteen Tales Of Terror
From The North Carolina Coast

Joe Sledge

Copyright © Joe Sledge/Gravity Well Books 2019
ISBN-13:978-0-9980968-3-4

First paperback edition 2019

Published by Gravity Well Books

For Callie

Table Of Contents

Introduction

Ghoulies and Ghosties are only a part of the things that go bump in the night along the thin ribbon of islands that comprise the Outer Banks. And it is little surprise that the land, and the sea, are so haunted that legends abound of the ghosts and spirits that pervade our coast. Life and death are close friends here. The tragedies of the past become part of our culture. They slowly work their way into our collective story.

The ghost stories of the Outer Banks have a special place in our hearts. They are close to fables, tales of sadness that remind us of what we should respect, and how we should or shouldn't act. Some merely are spooky tales that we like to tell to scare the little ones around the campfire, or use to set into motion an exploration of the old dark woods. They make the blood cool just a little, so that every shadow is a little darker, every breath a bit quieter and deeper. Others reach deeper into us. They are reminders of events, maybe

1

fancied up, but they were real, and they tell us what happened when someone didn't listen, someone got too mad, or strayed from the course of society. They become a wonderful mix of testing our limits, but knowing not to go too far.

Most people know the beginning of the quote at the start of this passage...

*From goulies and ghosties and long-leggedy beasties
And things that go bump in the night*

But not everyone knows the end, *Good Lord, deliver us!* The prayer is an old Scottish talisman, from the early 1900s, in hopes to keep all those unexplained fears and creatures in the dark from creeping onto their doorsteps and into their houses. Outer Bankers have met their fears with a little more fortitude, not shutting their doors to the things that go bump in the night. They keep a healthy respect, and maybe a healthy distance, for the ghosts of the coast.

So enjoy this collection of tales, some old chestnuts well told and worth retelling, and some new or lesser known, but just as fun.

Haunted Currituck Light

The barren coast of Corolla could do nothing to hold back the tide as it rose to kiss the dry sand of the shore. The few fishermen out along the beach knew that the tide was rising. They made a point to move back past the high tide line, marked by thin strings of sand and shells where the last waves had deposited them early that morning. Little Sadie Johnson didn't bother to move. Her sand castle was too important, too big, and too close to completion to leave it now. She was so intent on the last, tallest tower, that she paid no attention to the ocean crashing behind her.

A big wave rose up behind her. It was pushed and piled up, stacked higher and higher as the wave before it poured back into the ocean. With a crash and a rushing hiss, it slammed into the shore, putting its energy into moving up the beach. Too late, Sadie Johnson heard the wave rushing up the sand as she turned.

The wave rushed up around Sadie's ankles. It sloshed into her castle, digging it out from the bottom and knocking down the walls and towers she had worked so hard for.

Sadie turned to the ocean and began to scold it, tut-tutting with a stern finger, "You shouldn't do that! Don't knock my castles down, wave!" She worried less about her wet dress and how dangerously close she was to the ocean.

Far away, a local fisherman threw down his tackle and pole and ran to the girl. Once he finally got to her, he grabbed Sadie harshly by the arm. "Whot are you doin', choild?!" he yelled. "Git away from that ocean, girl. You cain't turn your back on the waves loike that!" He began pulling the girl up the beach toward the sandy dunes and the path back home.

Back to her father's home, the Currituck Lighthouse.

It was a long walk back and the fisherman wouldn't let go the whole way. Sadie's arm ached, and her shoulder was twisted in the old man's grip. Sadie didn't like it, but she wasn't worried about being in trouble. Her father was an assistant keeper at the light. And he loved the girl with every beat of his heart. George Johnson wasn't really Sadie's father. He was her uncle. But Sadie's real father had died when she was little, and she really only knew George as her daddy. He was always

4

kind and fun, very loving, never stern with her even as he set rules for the girl on the lonely empty island.

There was little to do for Sadie. She occasionally played with the other children on the island, though there were so few of them that she was often alone. Sadie made the best of her lonely life by playing on the beach, building sand castles until the waves knocked them down and she had to go in. Her father had told her, over and over, don't turn your back on the ocean, don't play near the waves, but Sadie didn't listen. She was too carefree, too wild, too much like the rest of the island to be tamed. She always thought she would push the waves back with a good talking to.

Sadie arrived at the lighthouse keepers' quarters, still locked in the fisherman's arm.

"Yer girl almost got worshed away agin," the fisherman scolded the keeper.

George gently took Sadie away from the rough man, picking her up in his arms gently. "Thank you, I'll take her inside and deal with her," George said. The old fisherman humphed, but couldn't get mad at the kind keeper. He was a nice man, and a good keeper. He was just soft on the child.

Now, Sadie," George said, in his strictest voice, which was still soft and warm to the little girl, "I've told you before, I've warned you about this. You need to stay away from the shore. You need to be more careful in the future. You've gotten your dress all wet. You need to care for your things. We can't get clothes here very easily." He patted the girl on the head as he set her down in the shadow of the home they shared with two other keepers, while the giant red brick lighthouse towered over her, the only sentinel along the northern part of the empty Outer Banks.

"Yes, father," she always agreed. And then always forgot the next time she went out.

The next day, when it was time for Keeper Johnson to go to work, Sadie did as she always did, wandered to the shore, and began building her sand castles. No one was on the beach to watch her this time. No one to remind her to not turn her back on the ocean, no one to scold her, no one to point out the rising tide. This time the waves took more than her castle.

By the time the family noticed that little Sadie was missing, the evening was drawing near. The sky turned a burned orange, casting a soft glow on the bricks of the lighthouse, and casting a long shadow out toward the beach. It reached out its dark hand, a long thin line over the yellow sand.

George and his wife searched the shore. Locals came out into the twilight, using whatever light they had. But it was for naught. The girl was nowhere to be found. Everyone knew she had been washed out to sea. The likelihood of her surviving was nil. No one lasted that long in the ocean, especially a little girl in a waterlogged dress. It would be days until Sadie's lifeless body would turn up farther north, near the Virginia border.

Sadie was brought back to the keeper's house and placed in her room, a small room on the north side, meant only for children or guests. This time, it would be for a short wake. Only a few people would come by to pay their respects; death was too common an occurrence and the islanders had little time for sorrow. A wake was usually meant to see if the deceased would awake from an illness, but this time everyone knew that the girl was well and truly dead. The salt water had taken her life quickly, and was as quickly taking her body.

Sadie would be wrapped and boxed up to be taken to her family's cemetery in Virginia for a prompt and hurried burial.

The room took on a notion of sadness, and would not be used for members of the Johnson family again. It would be years before anyone would even stay in the room, and then it would be for another sad and tragic affair.

Another keeper had brought his wife with him. The loneliness of the job meant that the keepers always benefited from a spouse in the home to keep the place warm and the food hot. Sadly, the wife would be unable to meet her side of those duties, as she came down with tuberculosis, a dreaded and deadly disease of the time. With no known cure, and a deep fear of the disease's communicable nature, the patient was usually just put away from others, tended to with a dispassionate respect of distance, and there they simply awaited a slow death.

Which is exactly what happened to the keeper's wife.

While she wasted away in the north room, Sadie's old room of life and death, the rest of the families went on with their lives. She sat on the bed or read what books she had, waiting for her food to be served at the doorway and the server to leave down the hall. While others clinked glasses and regaled with the tales of the day, she sat alone, getting thinner and thinner, her only conversation would be the ones she had with herself, coughing fits that said little and made no sense. They were arguments with herself that she would not win.

The woman would pass away in the room and be buried unceremoniously, in order to stave off spreading the disease. Her effects, all tainted by tuberculosis, were put away, sealed in a a large barrel, and the vat was left in the corner of the north room, with the unnecessary warning for most to stay out of the room.

The north room was closed off, a room of death, never intended to be opened. Even walking by the room people would have a pallor cast upon them, a feeling of dread and unease. The room was cold, uninviting. It would stay that way as the keepers' house was finally closed up and the lighthouse automated as it moved fully into the 20th century.

By the 1940s, the building sat unused, and presumably empty by the locals. Several of the children of Corolla would go to play in the courtyard, under the towering lighthouse, sending the ponies that fed on the wild grass around the old house scampering. Their parents didn't mind, but they warned the kids not to go into that old house. And definitely don't go into the North Room and play around that old barrel. It was diseased.

But the kids were kids, and they didn't listen. Or perhaps they listened to another voice. A childlike plea was heard from the old house, "Come play with me…" and the children did. They went to find the old barrel filled with the woman's clothes. They cracked it open through the staves, and pulled out the woman's fine clothing. Trying on the clothes, they played a macabre game of dress up as they wandered the abandoned house, all while adorned in the diseased apparel.

Sickened and repulsed, the parents of the village punished the children severely. The clothes were gathered up, along with the barrel, and burned to fine ash in the courtyard. The old keepers' quarters were again sealed. Any voices speaking out in the house talked only to themselves.

It would be decades before the keeper's house was ever cracked open again. When the first restorers entered the house in the 1980s, after over forty years of the old home being closed up, with whatever spirits locked up alone, too, many noticed a distinct feel, a sense of coldness, a morbid sad feeling in the North Room. As workers went about their tasks of restoration, many stated flatly that they wouldn't enter the room. It was too dark, too frightening. Guests staying the night in the North Room have had the sheets pulled off the bed, and in the quietest of times a voice has called out, "Come play with me…"

Joe Sledge

The Last Guests of Whalehead

In the 1920s, the Outer Banks was the vacation home for hundreds of thousands of travelers. A major highway ran right through the islands, and it was the perfect stopover for tourists looking for a place to rest, get a bite to eat, and spend time with their families.

It wasn't people that vacationed, though. It was birds. Migratory waterfowl stopped in the clean open waters on their way to or from their seasonal homes, escaping the cold of the north, or leaving the south as the temperature got warmer. With all the birds that rested in the waters, the area also brought hunters. Rich sportsmen from far up north escaped the cold by coming down to rustic hunting lodges up in Corolla to go out, shoot to their content, fish when they wanted, and rest by warm fires the rest of the day. It was perfect if you were a wealthy sportsman. It was impossible if you were a sportswoman. But a lot of money would solve that problem.

11

When Edward Collings Knight and his wife, Marie Louise Lebel Knight wanted to come down from their stately Rhode Island home to be free of the bitter winter up north, Edward was welcome, but women were forbidden in the all male clubs that dotted the Currituck shore. The Knights solved that problem easily enough by purchasing an old hunt club and refurbishing it to their own tastes. The former Lighthouse Hunt Club became a very distinguished and personal vacation home. It was renamed Corolla Island by the Knights. It was never meant to be a club, and only the invited guests ever got to use the extravagances the Knights brought to the building.

The place had electric lights, hot and cold running fresh and salt water, indoor plumbing, and an elevator, the first on the island. It was also sumptuously appointed with Tiffany lights, a Steinway piano, and a floor to ceiling pink kitchen with refrigerator. Every step was made for the Knights and their guests to have every comfort. So it would be expected that they would happily spend their winters in their elegant home. Which they did, right up until 1933, when they abruptly left after spending only three weeks in the house that year.

No one knows why the Knights left, but the house was sold soon after that, going through numerous owners, used as a barracks during World War II, and then finally receiving its famous name, The Whalehead Club, when it became a famous hunting and sporting retreat, owned by Ray Adams. He planned to develop the area into a posh vacation retreat, but with no roads to the area, those plans never were realized. He even tried to build an airplane runway. When he began to dig, he found a whale bone in the ground, giving rise to the name. Adams would live, and die, in the house in 1957. It was used as a school and later a rocket testing site until the early 1970s when it was sold and effectively abandoned.

It just may not have been empty all that time.

In the quiet in-between times, when the building was unused, the ghosts may have stirred when receiving unannounced visitors. Corolla local Norris Austin told of an early visit during a hurricane that hit Corolla. Austin's family wouldn't evacuate during the storm, a stubborn streak of many locals. The owner of the Whalehead Club at the time, Bill Witt, a real estate developer, told Norris to stay over at the house during the storm since it would be higher up and relatively safe. So Norris, along with his dog, found their way through the winds to the house and took refuge in an upstairs room. He set up a mattress on the floor, along with some food and water for him and his dog, and settled in for a nap.

He awoke with a start. His dog had started barking and growling at a dark corner in the house. But nothing was there. Not even a shadow, even as the storm grew in intensity. The wind whipped across the house, whistling like tiny screaming banshees trying to get in. But Norris didn't care about the storm outside. His dog was barking, snarling at something that only the dog could sense. Norris saw nothing in the room. He tried to calm his dog, but the poor pup was both angered and terrified, backed into a corner in a house with a raging hurricane outside and nowhere to go.

Norris immediately became concerned, and then scared. What could terrify his dog so much that wasn't even in the room? He decided he wouldn't find out. The storm was a safer harbor than what ever it was that his dog could sense be he couldn't see. Norris rode out the rest of the hurricane at his home.

When the club was a testing facility for rockets, sometimes the employees would bring their spouses down to the isolated beach for a short vacation and to watch some of the tests. That brought the wife of one man to the Whalehead Club. The couple spent the night in the Knights' bedroom since it was the most comfortable. In the middle of the night, the husband awoke to a creaking bathroom door. Figuring it was just the wind, the man got up to use the bathroom with the intent to wedge something under the door once he left. As he left the bathroom, he found his wife already at the task, kneeling down by the door. He quietly stepped around her in the dark. As he climbed back into bed, he found his wife already there, still sound asleep. She wasn't the woman kneeling at the door.

Even since its refurbishment, the club still has its haunts. Pots and pans rattle in an empty kitchen. Lights appear on security cameras in darkened rooms. The elevator operates even when it has no power to call it. Mysterious events happen in Mr. Knight's study, as guests have seen ethereal forms of men, huddled in a corner, discussing things in serious tones. When the visitors try to stare at them, the men turn away and vanish into nothingness. And Mr. Knight makes his presence known on occasion, by still enjoying a cigar in his room. Visitors swear they smell the sweet aroma of his cigars in the house, even though no one smokes inside the wooden building.

What may be the scariest haunt of the building is in the basement. Footsteps sound in the narrow hallway where no feet tread. A small girl has made herself known, grabbing at the ankles of a boy visitor. The corporeal boy ran screaming from the fingers of the ghostly girl, who called and begged to have someone play with her. She never appears anywhere else in the house. She seems to be trapped within the confines of the subterranean vault, always looking to escape, but never able to leave.

All of the haunts, the tales, the strange ethereal residents that have been seen, heard, and sensed, they all have one thing in common. They are completely unknown as to what may have caused them. All seem to have a tragic story behind them, but none of them are known to have a cause. The smoke in the study very well may be Mr. Knight, even though he only spent his winters in the house. The same with the strange presence in the bedroom being Mrs. Knight. But the others, the strange hidden demon that scared a poor dog out of its wits and drove a man into a storm, no one knows what that could be. And the little girl, all alone, trapped in a basement, begging to have someone play with her, well, that may best be a tale left untold and undiscovered.

Joe Sledge

The Ghost Of The Black Pelican

It is difficult today to picture a different life on the Outer Banks in the 1800s, with a nearly empty windswept beach, the islands smooth with no dune to stop the relentless waves that rolled over the shore and washed inland. The beaches were spotted with driftwood and seashells, with no beachcomber to collect the decorations in the sand.

There were other items that washed up that were uncommon, but sadly not rare enough. Shipwrecks would find the Outer Banks during storms. If the sailing ships were fortunate, it may only be a stranding on a sandbar. More likely, the ships were stuck hard and fast, the masts cracked and snapped, the hulls unrepairable, leaking, listing, ready to dump their contents into a cold and merciless sea. When it was

17

cargo, the losses were expensive. When it was people, the loss was so much worse.

Fortunately, groups of men guarded the shore. Rough, strong, and fearless, they were members of a tight knit community, the U.S. Life-Saving Service. While others might snuggle themselves into a warm cottage during the worst of storms, these men squared themselves against the weather that cast lost ships toward the shore or into a fickle and uncaring ocean.

This was a very accurate painting of the men who stood watch at the Kitty Hawk Lifesaving Station during the summer of 1884. And none were tougher than the Keeper, James Hobbs.

To say that Hobbs ran a tight ship would have been an understatement. He demanded perfection from his men, and he got it. He drilled and drilled until going out in a raging storm on the Atlantic was preferable to practice for his crew. The life saving crew had a great deal of respect for the man, but even the toughest of them had a little bit of fear for the wrath of James Hobbs.

There was one person who wasn't afraid of Hobbs, though. As a matter of fact, he hated the keeper with a passion. And that hatred would be T.L. Daniels undoing.

Captain Theopolis "T.L." Daniels had it in for Keeper Hobbs. He always looked for ways to pick a fight with Hobbs, from pointed and unveiled insults, done in public and around the crew, to directed attacks on Hobbs' wife. "One day you are going kill a whole crew with your actions!" he accused the keeper. "Those deaths will be on your head, and everyone will know it," Daniels went to every length to provoke Hobbs. He very publicly spit tobacco juice on the dress of Hobbs' wife, and insinuated that it did no harm to her looks.

Hobbs stewed in the summer heat. No one would blame him if he simply pummeled the old bully. Everyone suspected that Daniels wanted Hobbs' job, though all the life savers professed they would never work for the man. But Keeper Hobbs was as professional as he was tough. Daniels was an itch he couldn't scratch, no matter how much it irritated Hobbs. So Hobbs stewed, and Daniels stalked.

With summer coming on, Daniels spied Hobbs painting his boat, preparing it for the calm summer season. Daniels saw a way to get the man in trouble, and wrote away to the Life Saving Service, accusing Hobbs of using government owned paint on his personal boat. True or false, Daniels hoped to finally provoke Hobbs into a fight, and with a government audience in the form of Lt. E.C. Clayton of the Life Saving Service holding court at the station.

Clayton arrived in Kitty Hawk on July 7, 1884. He shifted uncomfortably in the heat, his glasses slipping down the front of his sweating nose, his collar too tight

19

for the heat of the day. His hope was to get this over with as quickly as possible. From the onset, he found Daniels irritating and ungracious. Clayton had already made up his mind as the accused and accuser, along with the surfmen, all gathered in the station for the hearing. Hobbs and Daniels glared, shooting lightning bolts of hate at each other in the small room, with Clayton in the middle, seated at a small table. The surfmen stood around the edge of the room, leaning against the walls.

"Do you have any evidence other than your accusation?" Clayton began the hearing with hopes that he could bring it to a quick end and escape the obvious tension of the room. Daniels didn't even hear the words; he was too busy glaring at Hobbs. Both sat on the edge of their seats, each ready to spring at the other, ready to tear at the other's throat.

"I know what you are thinking," Daniels accused Hobbs. "If you ever draw so much as a pen knife on me, I will kill you!"

"I don't have a weapon on me, you old fool," Hobbs spat back. "And we all know you have a pistol hidden in your pocket! If you try to draw out on me, it will be the last thing you do!"

Daniels couldn't take the insult, or the threat. He began to draw his pistol, a difficult action as he was seated. He pushed his chair back, his hand diving into his pocket and pulling. The barrel hung up on his pocket, and the hammer hooked under his coat.

Seeing the bloodlust rising, the crew began to scatter, running for the doors and climbing out the window. There was business to be done, and they wanted none of it. Only poor Lt. Clayton was caught in the middle with nowhere to go.

Keeper Hobbs, who had faced down much worse in his time, remained calm, but sprang into action. He stood up to open a nearby closet and removed a loaded double barreled shotgun he stored there. Daniels had almost cleared his pistol, and was trying to move backwards to get clear of Clayton in order to shoot Hobbs right between his hate filled eyes. Hobbs didn't worry about the lieutenant being in the way.

He simply stepped forward, laid the barrel across Clayton's shoulder, and fired.

The blast deafened Clayton in one ear, and sent him jumping up and over the table to escape, the ringing in his head only a distant concern over saving his life. Daniels was less fortunate.

The shotgun blast had struck him the shoulder, knocking him to the floor. His body tangled with the wooden chair he had sat in, turning him into a twisted and bloody mess. But he was still alive. His pistol was cleared now, and he rose the weapon shakily to take aim and deal back some damage.

Hobbs cocked his shotgun, and with a smirk, fired his second barrel into Daniels.

When it was all over, what seemed like minutes but was really just seconds, the small office was now a bloody abattoir. The last of T.L. Daniels' life poured out onto the wooden floor, staining the planks crimson with his blood. Hobbs called his men back in, "That fellah is done here," he proclaimed, and everyone believed him.

Lt. Clayton and the life saving crew all agreed that Daniels' undoing was all his own fault. Hobbs had been unarmed, hadn't threatened Daniels, and Daniels had come in armed with a plan to kill Hobbs. The execution came before the judge and jury, but the result was the same, they decided. The old man's remains were gathered as best as they could be, and the crew took what was left of Daniels and threw him into the deep sea, having left the world no poorer for his absence.

What would be merely a macabre tale of death and mayhem long lost and forgotten hasn't ended with Daniels' death. The Life Saving Service changed into the Coast Guard, and the old building sat abandoned for a long time, used as a house, and finally picked up and moved away from the shore. The building that was part of saving so many lives was now itself saved and given new life.

It was converted into the Black Pelican Restaurant, a usually lively and popular place to eat and drink. But lively may not necessarily mean alive.

The ghost of T.L. Daniels still haunts the old station, now the Black Pelican. His blood stains remain in the wood floor near the entrance, a permanent marker of where he fell from his wounds and bled out. At night, when the restaurant is closed and the staff are filtering out, a lone figure, smoky, cloudy, ethereal, has been seen sitting in a corner of the restaurant. The walls have been seen to bleed, as if the sanguine splatter of Daniels' last life came back through to present day. Unearthly appearances or cold, distressing spots have been felt in the bathrooms and stairways. It is thought that, due to his arrogance, and his hard headedness, T.L. Daniels is cursed to remain where he died. He still longs for the job he wanted and respect he desired, but must serve a penance for a life taken over by envy and desire.

Ghosts In The Mists

If the 1960s had done anything to the Outer Banks, Marcie Elliott hadn't seen much of it yet. She had finally turned 13, "Technically a teenager," she had argued, in hopes of escaping the old beach house and be allowed to prowl more of the beach, hopefully to spend some time with her older sister who always seemed to have all the fun. She got to go down the road to the Casino, or hike up Jockey's Ridge with her friends. Marcie, however, had to spend her days around the old beach house belonging to her grandfather, Doc.

The house was truly old. Marcie had heard the term "Unpainted Aristocracy" used to refer to the house, and all the neighboring houses, but she found nothing aristocratic about the house. It was old, wooden, it shook when it rained, and leaked some, too. It got hot in the day, and really hot when it stormed and they closed the windows, which she didn't understand why, because, well, the house leaked anyway. At least leave the windows open. The postcards of the new motels with air conditioned rooms and sparkling blue pools looked so much more aristocratic than her grandfather's place. The bouncy beds with clean sheets, no sand in them, were fancier than the one in her room. She would spend her nights on top of the sheets, listening to the ocean waves lull her to sleep as they rhythmically crashed upon the shore.

Well, maybe that part wasn't too bad.

So, the house was old, wooden, it smelled of salt and ocean and a bit of tobacco. It was covered with sand that piled up wherever it could, especially underneath the house. Marcie liked playing under the house. It was cool and dark, hidden from the adult world above. There was always something to discover down there. Only last year she had found the trap door in the floor of the beach house. Her grandfather had explained that the house sat on pilings and long ago it would be lifted off to move it away from the shore when a hurricane came. But if the storm came too fast, they would just open the trap door and let the water to wash in and weigh the house down so it wouldn't float away. It was all nailed down now. Nothing was coming in that way anymore.

Marcie thought that was a foolish reason to seal up a perfectly good trap door.

So she spent her mornings on the beach, with only a quick visit to the beach house for a lunch her mom made her, then back out for more swimming, more visiting with the neighbor kids, looking longingly at the older teens who would find a way to wander off in the afternoons and evenings to explore Jockey's Ridge or go dance the evening away. She ended up on the back porch, or less often now, under it, in the cool shade under the house.

That was where she was, one afternoon, noticing that one side of the house was distinctly less covered with sand than in the past. She heard her parents thumping above, causing thin gauzy clouds of dust and sand to fall from above her. The pilings were surrounded by cheap slats of wood. Her grandfather explained it was to keep the pigs out. She always laughed at that. There were no pigs in Nags Head.

The lower sand allowed her to wander over to that side of the house, near the only stone foundation, where the fireplace rested. There was an old gate there, now nailed closed and half buried, where people used to crawl underneath the house, maybe to get to the fireplace, Marcie guessed. She could see the old latch, a simple piece of wood on a nail, to turn to open and close. Then she noticed something else. Nearby, on the bottom slat, something was attached. It was a long board, thicker but narrower than the cheap wood nailed to the pilings. Marcie crawled through the sand to see what it was. She had never seen the board before since it was covered in sand up until that day.

It was nailed at each end to the plank, There was no space to pull the board, and Marcie didn't want to break anything. Crawling back out, she called up to her father, "Daddy, where's the hammer?" The tools of the beach house, probably all beach houses like this, resided in a dusty magic box somewhere under the stairs or in the carriage house. The box usually had a hammer, a drill, several screwdrivers that were never the right size for the job, and a myriad collection of nails in jars. She wandered to the little garage, originally meant to hold a horse drawn wagon, Marcie guessed, where she found the Pandora's Box of old tools.

"In the tool box!" her father yelled distantly.

"..."

"Why?"

"Never mind!" Marcie screamed back. Her father would almost immediately go back to not caring what happened to anyone on the entire island as he sipped tea from a sweaty glass.

Back underneath in a flash, she crawled over to the wood attachment. It was different, she could tell by the ends which were curved and scrolled. Someone had put this there long ago, but it was not part of the house. If nothing else, it was a nice decorative bit of wood. She began prying...

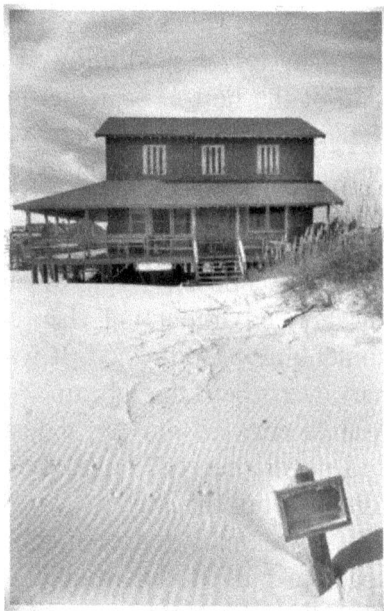

"Hey, Momma, d'you know what the name *Alston* means?"

Marcie's mom was not doing anything, which was almost a surprise to Marcie. She usually was washing dishes or cooking or one of many things that she seemed to want to escape from when she came to the beach from Elizabeth City. "Hmmm? What? Uh, *Alston*? Is it supposed to?"

Marcie walked in the side door to the kitchen carrying the long wood plank. She had only seen the back side, she discovered. On the other side, hidden as it was attached to the planks under the house, it was painted and carved, as if to protect the lettering. In heavy nautical paint, over chiseled letters was the word *Alston*. "Yeah, look, look what I found in the sand under the house," Marcie wasn't going to tell that she had actually removed it. It might have been important down there.

"Where did you find that?!" her mother didn't hear what Marcie just said. "Wait, under the house? What is it? Bob? Bob!" she yelled for her husband on the back porch. "Come look at this! Look at what Marcie found!"

Marcie's father had no intention to get up out of his rocking chair. "What is it?"

"Come see!"

Vacation wasn't meant to be getting up and all that, Bob thought. His eyes lit up some when he saw the old board with the writing on it. "Where did you find that?!"

"It was under the house," Marcie beamed with pride at her discovery. "What is it? What's an *Alston*?"

"Not what, but probably who. Well," thought Bob, "Maybe more a *she*. It's a quarterboard for a ship.

"An old one, too."

The day of discovery slowly blended into an afternoon of contentment and rest. Marcie relaxed on the back porch with her father until it got dark enough that the sun set behind Jockey's Ridge and the ocean turned a deep dark blue. The sky went from orange to purple to almost black as the waves crashed slowly onto the shoreline. The first stars twinkled on over the horizon in the night. The soft ocean waves had a faint glow from

27

plankton being churned in the shorebreak. Almost imperceptibly, Marcie thought she heard whispers and the soft tinkle of metal, almost like her sister's bracelets rattling as she walked.

Just as Marcie stood up to look out over the beach, her father came out. "Marcie, time to come in!" Marcie took one last glance at the beach where she half saw, half imagined some people walking in the dark. But it was bedtime. Nights on the beach may be short, but they offered little to do on the Outer Banks. A few minutes of staticky AM radio and Marcie was yawning, unable to keep her eyes open.

The next morning, the sky was dreary, gray and overcast. Marcie was up early, eating a bowl of cold cereal. Looking out over the beach, with the sand a dull brown, she could see that the sand had been swept clean from a recent morning rain, except for one place just above the high tide line where shells and dead sea flea carcasses littered the sand. There a strange path of footprints occurred, like a line of people had shuffled from one point to another along the beach by her grandfather's house.

It was a long morning with no real way to get outside when the rain came in fits and the skies never cleared. Marcie's sister walked around the house in a dark mood. She couldn't get out to see her friends, and there was nothing to entertain her in the beach house. Marcie had looked forward to her grandfather coming down from Elizabeth City. He always entertained her with stories and adventures around the beach. She hoped to ask him about the sign she found. Marcie was disappointed when she heard her mom say, "Granddaddy called, he's not coming down today with all the wind and rain. He said he will come tomorrow."

So Marcie moped around, too. Cheap novels and old ghost tale books moved to jigsaw puzzles with pieces missing. The day got long, and then the day got dark.

Marcie sat on the back porch again, watching the sea oats droop under the rain. Again she watched the waves churn onto the shore, and she waited for the darkness to see if the waves would glow again.

In the dim last rays of twilight, under a purple and gray sky, Marcie saw some people walking in the rain. She was surprised, and watched them surreptitiously. They walked in a line, heads down against the rain, like they were looking for shells or sea glass. But they never looked up, never where they were going. It looked like they would get caught and washed away in the waves, but the water never quite touched them.

Marcie stood up, slowly and quietly. There was something odd about them, something just wrong. Then she noticed what was bothering her.

The wind was blowing their clothes, like it should. Coats, dresses, whatever they were, they were being pulled by the wind as it blew to the sea.

But the figures blew with the wind, too.

It was like they were made of smoke, or fog, with bits pulling away and coming back. They weren't all there.

Marcie's blood went cold and her heart skipped a beat, turning it heavy like lead in her chest. There was no way that she was seeing what she was seeing, but the figures were real. As real as the gauzy clouds of people could be.

"Daaaaaad…" Marcie called, a half whisper, half plea.

The figures all stopped, as if to turn and look at the sound. How could they hear her from there, in a storm? Marcie wondered.

Her father came out the screen door with a screech of the spring and a slam of the frame. "What, honey?" he asked.

Marcie looked back at her father, and out to the purple twilight, just as the figures disappeared into smoke.

"I… I thought I saw some people out there…"

Marcie's sleep was fitful. She tossed and turned, worried about ghostly figures on the beach. The next morning the weather was clear, the skies were blue with early clouds streaking lazily in the atmosphere. With the sun going from orange sunrise to yellow morning, Marcie walked out of the house and down to the beach, cresting over the low dunes. The sand was clear and beaten from the storm, except up to the line of dunes by her house. There she clearly saw the footprints of people, many people. They seemed to lead from and to the ocean.

Marcie looked far to the north and south, seeing a few fishermen out early to catch bluefish for the day. She wasn't sure if she wanted to go to the beach today.

Marcie walked over to Jockey's Ridge, ate lunch at the nearby restaurant, and generally wandered the roads, watching the cars go by on the new bypass. The one thing she didn't want to do was go home and wait for dark, but she had little other choice.

Marcie was elated to walk back to the house and see a new car in the sand covered drive. The brown Chrysler meant only one thing, her grandfather had come down.

Marcie adored her grandfather, and looked forward to any chance to hear his stories or spend time with him. She could ask him about the people on the beach. Her grandfather had been coming to the beach since the turn of the century, and had seen the changes had come to the beach. The old beach house had belonged to his grandfather before him, and he should know all the secrets that came with it.

Marcie rushed in the door, "Grandfather!" she called. She found him, her mom, and her father, all in the old living room, standing by the brick fireplace, long unused in the seasonal home. The three were standing together in a suspicious huddle, while her grandfather looked over her find, the mysterious sign *Alston*, which they had propped over the mantle. His grave look gave way to a smile as he saw his favorite grandchild.

"What's up, Duck?!" he greeted Marcie. She answered back, "What's up, Doc?"

Marcie giggled at the greeting they always had. As a little girl, she got a kick out of how people never called her grandfather by his name, Milton, but always "Doc," since he was a pharmacist. She thought they called him "Duck" and the nickname stuck.

"Did you see what I found?! Daddy said it was a...a..."

"It's a quarterboard, the nameplate of a ship," Doc said. "You found this under the house?"

"Yes," she said, adding a soft lie to the statement, "It was buried in the sand." Which was technically true.

"Where's it from, Doc?" asked Marcie's mom. "Is it really from an old ship? Like a shipwreck?"

"Well..." Doc scratched his head. It was going to be hard to explain. "You know how long ago, there used to

31

be land pirates here, right? The old legend of Nags Head, and how they would lead a horse with a lantern on its neck up and down the hills, making it look like a ship in a harbor, so the other ships would beach themselves. Well, the old Nags Head lantern on Jockey's Ridge probably isn't true." Marcie was surprised. She had seen the souvenir nag statue in the nearby Forbes candy shop for so long it became second nature to believe the tale. Doc saw her surprised face.

"It would have burned the horse's neck. And no horse would put up with that. They'd run wild."

Marcie had never thought of that. It seemed cruel, even to an old nag.

"Anyway, the old land pirate stories are true. And so were all the shipwrecks. Whenever a ship would strand itself and be abandoned, the locals would go and take everything off it they could use, even strip the wood off for their houses. There was so little wood here except driftwood for fires. A lot of these houses have pieces of ship wood in their foundations."

Doc thought for a moment, "You know, I think I have a blanket made out of an old ensign or flag somewhere. The old ladies would take the cloth they found and stitch them up for comforters.

"Under the house, huh?" he looked quizzically, and concerned, at Marcie. "They say that the beaches around here are still haunted by the shipwrecked sailors and passengers that were lost at sea. If there were still passengers on board, then the ships couldn't be salvaged. So some of the early residents just did the easy thing and threw them overboard. Made'em walk the plank, so to speak."

Marcie found this both delicious and horrible. She loved old tales of pirate legends, but the blood and death always sent shivers down her spine. She looked at Doc with relish at the tale, but he seemed dead serious.

"Well, let's just leave this where it is," he said as he put the quarterboard back on the mantle. "Don't want to stir up the ghosts, do we?"

That afternoon, Marcie walked the beach with Doc. She had decided to confide in her grandfather the events she witnessed. "Tell, me something, Doc, was that story you said true? About the ghosts on the beach?"

"Well, sweetie, I don't know for sure. I've seen some strange things here, I'll tell you that. See that old house down there?" he pointed far to the south, past Jockey's Ridge, to another old house in the Unpainted Aristocracy. "I was in there as a kid. And I swear I saw someone in the kitchen door. A figure in all black, just standing there, out of the corner of my eye. But when I turned to look, there was nothing there at all.

"And then the kitchen door closed slowly, all on its own." His face gave away no hint that he was joking.

"What about the ghosts, on the beach?"

"Why do you ask?" he inquired of the girl.

"It's just, well, 'cause I saw people down here the past two evenings, in the rain, when people shouldn't really be out. And they didn't look all there." She looked to see if her grandfather would laugh at her.

He didn't. But he wasn't sure what to say to her, either.

"We may just have to be on the lookout tonight, then," he said simply.

The two were conspiratorially silent about their plans for the rest of the evening. Doc told tales of the old houses, what he found on the beach as a kid, digging up shipwrecks, being chased away by the local natives when he went exploring. They pulled up the old rug to see the trap door, and Doc showed some old pictures of a house being pulled from the ocean side by a team of ten horses. It was all so amazing to Marcie that she almost forgot what she was worried about. By the time darkness rolled in over the ocean, they had not even bothered to look out on the beach for people, ghostly or live.

"Well, time for me to go to bed," Marcie's dad yawned sleepily. "C'mon, honey," he held his hand out for his wife, who just started feeling her eyes droop. "You staying up, Dad?" he asked his father.

"Yup, for a little bit. You go on, me an' Marcie are gonna go look at the ocean in the moonlight one time. Just waiting 'til we turn out the lights."

The house slowly settled in for the night, and everything got dark. Then the moonlight filtered in through the windows, soft and blue. Marcie and Doc walked out to the dune. "Now, let's see what we can see," he whispered. Marcie couldn't tell if her grandfather was serious, or this was just another adventure for the old man.

They looked out over the dunes, through the sea oats that scattered here and there, but they saw nothing. Not at first. It was just the soft crush of the small ocean waves as they kissed the shore and ran up the sand pebbles.

"So... they say that the ghosts of those shipwrecked sailors are just looking for their ships, just wanting to get to their destination."

"You ever see them, Doc? Here on the beach?"

"Nah," he said. "In that house, once, but on the beach, nope." He looked out to sea. "Maybe we scared them aw..." Doc stopped before he could finish. Along the shore he could see the white of the small waves against the black ink of the ocean, the moon lighting up the far away horizon. Then he noticed how spots of the white were getting fuzzy, darker.

It took just a moment for the two, the old man and young girl, to see them, but when the ghosts formed on the shore line, they knew what they saw. Marcie clung tight to her grandfather's arm, which was cold and rigid. Marcie couldn't tell, but he was as afraid as she was.

Then the ghosts started moving toward the hill.

They were not formless, they had a basic shape, but it was as if they were just smoke or fog. They were vaguely human, with legs and arms and heads, but no detail. In the darkness they had no faces visible.

"C'mon, Doc," Marcie tugged on his arm, "Let's go back!"

Doc agreed wordlessly. The two stumbled and ran back over the dunes, tripping over the dips and hills, until they got to the porch and then inside the door. Doc bolted the door, turned the deadlock, and snapped the doorknob lock as well. They moved to the middle of the room, looking out through the large salt covered glass window over the dining room table.

"What were..." Marcie started to whisper.

"Shhh!" Doc hissed to her. They couldn't see out into the darkness well, and he had no idea if the strange spirits were climbing over the dunes at this moment. Nothing happened for the longest time. Half imagined sounds of scruffling and squeaking came from far off. No one else was awake by now.

A soft thump came from under the house. Marcie jumped with a start, yelping and covering her mouth in fear her screams might give her away. She felt her blood go cold.

"They're under the house."

At that moment, they heard a creak and soft bang, and felt the floor move. In the moonlight streaming through the window, they could see where the old rug had been rolled back, exposing the trap door. It was nailed shut and sealed.

Yet it moved.

The door budged, just a crack, as if something pushed against it. The nails held tight, but squeaked a little under the pressure. Then it thumped again, harder. The moonlight went behind a cloud, darkening the light from outside.

Doc gave up any facade of bravery and went to turn on the light. If anything was coming in his house, he was at least going to see it. He switched on the light over the dining table, lighting up the room, and casting a dull orange haze over the downstairs and outside porch. The glow illuminated the outside just enough for them to see the figures, crowded onto the porch, looking in. Black on black forms, like smoke but thick, all stood out looking in the window, wanting in. The thumping got louder underneath the house. Marcie was terrified beyond speech, silently begging the ghosts to go away, and hoping her grandfather would do something.

But Doc had no idea what to do. He stood frozen to the spot, close to the door and window, hand still on the light switch. The ghosts shook and twisted, like a storm wind blew them, but stayed in one place. Then, in unison, they all opened their eyes.

Yellow eyes glowed, peering into the house, looking for something. Not focusing on Marcie nor Doc, they looked right past the two humans. The ghosts just stood there, watching and looking with their terrifying yellow eyes in black fog faces.

The only thing Doc could think to do was to turn on all the lights. It was a natural reaction to fear. Light, fire, day, they all opened the eyes of people to all they feared that went bump in the night.

Doc switched on the outside porch light.

The bright yellow glow of the lamp, meant to keep bugs from swarming, was a welcoming contrast to the eerie stare the wraiths had thrown at the two people. For a fleeting moment, they saw the ghosts clearly, clothes torn, disheveled, their bodies waterlogged and pasty from drowning in a cold merciless ocean long ago. Their faces were an ashy gray, the color of storm clouds, eyes sagging and bloodshot from an eternity of salt water.

And then they vanished, wisps of smoke disappearing into the ether.

"What did... we see, Doc?" Marcie was close to crying now, a mixture of relief and uncomprehension filling her cold veins.

"I don't know, honey... But I have an idea."

The next morning the family found Doc and Marcie, asleep, Marcie sprawled over the sofa and Doc snoring, asleep on his back, in his recliner chair. When they woke up, Doc put on a smile, saying they had stayed up to look for ghosts, a wink to his son and daughter in law, what seemed like a lie to cover up what was really the truth.

Doc took off right after breakfast, with a sip of coffee and an offhand, "I'll be back soon!" which didn't help Marcie in the least. He didn't come back until after lunch, but he smiled and said he had a story.

"So, I went talked to my friend David up in Southern Shores. He and some of his pals helped me out with the history of this thing," he pointed to the quarterboard on the mantle. "The *Alston* was a sailing ship that set sail to South Carolina sometime in the early 1800s. It was coming back loaded with rice, cotton, wood, rum from Jamaica, and a load of passengers heading to New York. It never even made it to Norfolk. Last time it was seen was heading past Cape Lookout. Most thought she was lost in a storm."

Marcie's father was only mildly interested by this time. It was ancient history now, just an old bit of a shipwreck long forgotten. "It musta washed up in a storm and gotten buried here, until you found it, huh, kid?" he smiled at his younger daughter, who gave back little in return.

Marcie wondered what her grandfather was going to do about the ghosts they saw last night. She knew the family wouldn't believe her unless the ghosts walked in and shook everyone awake. Which seemed likely after last night. Marcie thought they would just go home, but no one else even knew. Her grandfather pulled her aside once the others had left.

"I think I know what those ghosts want," he said simply. And he explained their plan. They could even do it right under the noses of the rest of the family and no one would be the wiser.

That afternoon, Marcie and Doc crawled under the house, "just to check it out," Doc explained. But really they looked for any old wood, anything that looked more like a ship that a house. They only found a few bits that seemed different than the usual local timber. Doc made sure he could remove them without the house falling in, and took them out to the sandy backyard.

The two gathered some scrap wood from a pile next to the house, and Doc set forth to built a boat. It wasn't big, barely five feet long, and only marginally like a boat. But it would float. "Just for some fun," he explained to his son, who went back to the beach for some afternoon fishing.

Doc even went up to the storage closet and found an old blanket that he was told was made from cloth found on a ship, like he had told the tale of before. He fashioned it into a crude sail. Finally, he affixed the old quarterboard to the side. It was about as long as the boat, and jutted off at a little bit of an angle, but that didn't matter. "Good enough for guvment work," Doc proclaimed. Marcie didn't know what that meant, but as long as it helped get rid of the ghosts, she didn't care. "Now what?" she asked.

"Now... we wait," Doc said firmly.

"It's gotta be dark,"Doc explained. He and Marcie stood at the beach in the twilight. It was still a bit orange, without all the purple that would fill the sky as night came on.

"How are we going to get it out there?" Marcie asked. She assumed they would float the model ship, but it would never get past the breakers, no matter how small the waves were.

"I'll just have to swim it out," Doc said.

"You sure you wanna do that, Doc? With those ghosts out there?"

"They don't want us, honey. Remember how they looked into the house? They weren't looking for us. They are looking for their ship. You uncovered it, it's not your fault," he reassured the crestfallen look on Marcie. "But they need to be set free. We're just going to help them on their way."

And with that, it seemed the world turned off its lights. The sky got dark as the last of the sun sank below the horizon, far behind Jockey's Ridge. "That's my cue, I guess."

Doc took off his shirt, now undressed down to only his shorts. He almost looked more like Surfer Joe than her grandfather, and she suppressed a laugh in spite of the situation. Doc reached into his pocket and pulled out a lighter. He lit a small candle stuck on the boat, hoping he could keep it lit through the water. Handing the lighter to Marcie, he held the model ship high and waded into the softly splashing waves.

Marcie watched him go, easily following the yellow candle as it wavered out past the breakers into deeper water. Finally Doc got out far enough that he had to tread water and push the boat along.

Then Marcie heard them. There was almost a collective voice, some strange murmur. She wanted to be close to the shore, be near her grandfather, but she couldn't be close to where those ghouls would come out after her. She backed up into the soft dry sand, nearer the dunes.

She could still see the candle lighting the boat far out in the ocean now. Then she saw the ghosts. They came ashore as if on a wave, the black smoke figures stood in a row. It seemed like there were fifty of them. Marcie fought not to run. Doc was out there, in the ocean, swimming, with nowhere else to go. The moon wasn't even up yet; it would take another hour to bring light to the situation.

Marcie saw the figures take a step toward her, toward the beach, toward the house. Then stop. They turned, and as if they were made of spun sugar, melted into the waves. She could see the black cloud sink into the water, darker than the surrounding greenish blue of the Atlantic. The cloud moved toward the little boat.

And Doc.

"Ooooohhh, Doc, get back," she whispered, afraid to shout.

Then the little ship caught the wind and began to sail. A warm southern wind pushed it out and away, heading it into deep water northward. It was like a magical kiss of wind, a breath to push the little boat away. It zipped off toward Kill Devil Hills.

And the cloud followed until it caught up, and disappeared.

Marcie felt a strange relief. It was a gust of happiness that flowed over her all of a sudden. The normally humid air of the beach was for a moment cool, dry, and graced with a sweet saltiness. And then it stopped.

Out from the ocean a black figure raised up, out of the water. Marcie became scared again, worried that one of the ghosts hadn't made it to their ship.

"Let's go in, girl. I need a towel, that water's cold."

The next morning everyone commented about how well they all slept that night.

Joe Sledge

The Hoodoo At The Dock

Johnny Wescott stood at the beginning of his family pier, which jutted out seemingly forever over the shallow tidal flats into the Roanoke Sound. He, his twin brother Scott, their friend Tommy Austin, and his cousin, Timmy Scarborough, younger than their age of 13 by a scant 3 years, barely 10, all waited as the sky darkened into a starlit night over the water. A thin and hazy crescent moon barely lit the water through the shimmering evening air. It was just enough to see where they stepped as they walked along the loamy sand of Roanoke Island's inland shore. The pier stuck out into the sound far enough that the water was deep enough for a small boat to sail away without running aground. Most of the dock was above a dry packed jetty of sand that had accumulated over the years as the currents twisted along the pier's pilings.

Tonight they were not going sailing. It was too good a night to do that. Still warm for early October, and a Friday to boot, it meant that the kids could stay out late. So tonight they would play with the hoodoos.

The kids had all heard of the hoodoos. Mysterious creatures that lived in the old house down the way on Mother Vineyard Road, hoodoos were small ghostly shapes, black garbed clouds or stooped over witches that lived in a chimney and came out at midnight. They haunted Mother Vineyard Road with complete indifference to the humans that dotted the forested land and natural shore. It was their world at night, the humans just slept in it.

Mother Vineyard Road was full of old tall tales. The boys had looked for and acted out every single one, trying to scare their friends from school, all the kids who hadn't experienced the ghosts and haints of Roanoke Island. There was a phantom bike rider that would pedal the road at night, casting an eerie glow as he rang his bell to pass. There's the old Etheridge ghost that haunts the house over by their family cemetery. And there were always rumors of a ghost haunting a tree where a Civil War paymaster was buried after being murdered for his gold.

But the boys always scoffed at the old legends. They liked playing hoodoo, though.

The game was simple, but still scary fun. One boy would stand on the dock, walking out as far as he dared, the older boys did it with their eyes closed, shuffling off so they didn't fall over the side into the shallow water. Once he stood still, the others, armed with flashlights, would scurry off into the darkness, their beams slicing through the underbrush of scuppernong and honeysuckle. Then the lights would go out. And the hoodoos would show up.

There would be a slight knocking on the pilings near the shore. Then it would get quiet. Then a shuffle of soft, almost imaginary, foot falls on the wet sand. If the boy opened his eyes, he might catch a glimpse of the dark figures scampering under the dock. Then the game would begin.

At the end of the dock, in the shallow water, there would be a solid thump. It would resonate through the dock, right to the boy's feet. Then another, one deck slat closer. Then another. Each closer and closer to the boy. The farther out he went, the closer he started to the hoodoos, the sooner he ran back to the safety of the grass. The closer to the shoreline, the longer it took for the hoodoos to slowly walk toward him, but the land was nearby. The bravest boys would try to go out the farthest, wait the longest.

Timmy had gone first. Egged on by the older kids, he had gone when the sky still held the slimmest of twilight. They had urged him to go sooner, as there would be fewer hoodoos out. Anxious to prove himself to his older cousins, he had done so, but eyes wide open and feet shuffling flat right down the center of the dock. The lights had gone out, and a lone hoodoo had chased Timmy in with little effort.

The older kids cheered him heartily. "You did better than I did when I was a kid," Johnny commended his little cousin. "That was the hard part, don't worry. Now you get to go hide and scare up the hoodoos for us." Timmy grinned happily at being part of the club.

Now it was fully dark, and it was Johnny's turn. He had waited until the night was out, without a sliver of light showing. He was the bravest, the most daring, he would stand right up to the end of the dock, where the hoodoos didn't like him to be. And he would walk back the slowest. And tonight would be no different than any other night, he vowed. Tommy always laughed and gave in, running back in delighted shivers at being scared out of his mind. Johnny's brother Scott would go out, but always gave in, coming back at a slow trot with his eyes wide open, like it was no big deal. But Johnny, he always made the kids under the dock, the "hoodoos," earn it.

He stood at the start of the pier, looking out over the long dock that reached into the inky water. Then, to add a bit of the dramatic, he turned around, looked at the three kids clutching their flashlights for protection against the monsters in the dark, closed his eyes, and stepped backward onto the wood planks. Johnny spun around on his heel to face forward. Cheating, he squinted to make sure he was pointed in the right direction, and began his walk to the end.

He knew how many steps he could take to get near the end, and the dock gave him a few clues, a soft board here, a squeak or creak there. He got about halfway before he peaked a look. No one could tell if he was looking, not this far out. He was still pretty straight, near the middle of the pier, and about fifty feet from the end. He couldn't go all the way out. Those were the rules. The hoodoos needed to be able to get out to the end, at least near the end, so they could start pushing back from under the pier. Johnny could always hear his friends under the dock, no matter how quiet they tried to be. It was part of the fun, to know they were there, and to wait for the first knock.

He got to the end of the walk, about 25 feet from the end of the pier. He could hear the *lap..lap..lap..* of the sound on the pilings farther out. And now he waited.

Thunk...

The hollow thump was almost immediate to Johnny stopping his feet. He was surprised that they got out there already, and he hadn't heard them. He turned around, beginning to speak, "Hey, guys, I'm not even ready y..." his voice droned off as he stared at the grassy hill on the shore, where the dock met the land. The wild vines of honeysuckle mixed with thick wild berry branches and small scrubby trees lounged lazily in the still air. In the opening between the bushes, clear as can be, burned the yellow bulbs of flashlights.

One.

Two.

Three.

All three boys still stood at the end of the dock. They hadn't even moved yet to run to the shore and get under the dock.

Thunk..

Johnny turned back to the water. It was louder this time. It came from the end of the dock. Where no kid was.

Thunk.

Closer still. It was loud, and heavy. Not like the soft clicks and thumps of kids.

Johnny took a step backwards.

Thunk... thunk...

There was something out there, and it wasn't one of his friends. They were all at the other end of the pier. No one had gone out in the time they had been there. Johnny didn't know what was under the dock.

What was under the dock?

Two more steps, no, three, he thought.

ThunkThunk

Johnny turned around. "What's going on?" he yelled. Who was messing with him?

THUNK!

That one was close. Maybe five boards away from him. Johnny started to run.

"What?!" Scott called. "What is it?" he never saw his brother like this before. They were just getting ready to head off to the beach, to switch off their lights and go be "hoodoos" once more into the night.

Then poor Johnny Wescott was on his toes running toward them.

And then they heard it.

ThunkthunkThunkThunkTHUNKthunkthunk…

Every step of Johnny Wescott was echoed by a horrible pounding beat. They shone their lights at Johnny, his face with a look they had never seen before. A look of fear. Of terror.

The three boys took off before Johnny even got to the beginning of the pier and hit the soft grass at a dead run. It took about ten feet for Johnny to catch them, pass them, and cross the empty road. He jumped the shrub that lined his home's property, not even touching the bristly leaves and twigs. The two older boys jumped, less gracefully but fully without care. Little Timmy had to run around to the opening, a terrifying few seconds where he felt the black hands of monsters reaching out in the darkness, his back bent in an unnatural angle to keep as much of him away from the reaching fingers of death that he imagined. He squealed in terror as he swung around the bushes and onto his cousins' property.

The boys didn't stop there. Up the stairs they ran, yanking mercilessly on the screen door, Johnny got there first. He pulled each of his friends in by the arm, and then pulled the screen door shut, locking it with a hook into an eye.

The boys breathed heavily. First they were afraid at what happened. Then, Johnny became ashamed. He was the brave one. This wasn't supposed to happen to him. Tommy spoke for them all, breaking the silence. "What was that? Who was out there?!" He was scared, but he didn't like being frightened in public, even in the dark. Someone had played a prank on them, and they had fallen for it.

"I dunno," Johnny panted. "First there was no one out there, and then…" he finally looked back up, out to the dock now far away, but still not far enough.

There, in the dark, by the sliver moon, they could see. First one shape, a black cloud, short, fat, wallowed up onto the pier. Then another, farther out, pulled itself up out of the sand and rose up on a piling. Then more. The dock became covered with hoodoos. Real ones, black hazy forms that swarmed the wooden pier, scampering about, looking for something only they could see with lifeless black eyes.

The boys would test their flashlights that night after they went to bed. The batteries would last all the way until morning.

Joe Sledge

The Legend Of The White Doe

A vineyard horticulturalist, Mark Daniels always said as he corrected people. Not a grape grower.

Mark thoroughly enjoyed his job as a horticultural expert on grapes and vineyards. About the only thing he didn't like was having to explain that he didn't grow grapes, or make wine, or have a vineyard.

He knew that certain grapes would grow just about anywhere in the state, so long as the soil was decent. The wonderful Scuppernong, sweet on the inside, dry on the outside, grew like a weed. As a matter of fact, about the only thing that would inhibit the Scuppernong was weed killer.

Which led him to his current job. Someone clearing power lines had sprayed an herbicide on a vine. And not just any vine, but the most famous grape vine in all of North Carolina, the Mother Vineyard.

The old twisted vine hung from a trellis out on Mother Vineyard Road on Roanoke Island. It had grown so big that someone with the power company mistook it for a weed and sprayed it to keep it back, not knowing he was killing the oldest planted vine in the United States.

Or so the legend goes.

Mark knew the basics of the legend. Supposedly, the vine was planted by the Lost Colony, the first English settlers to the New World, who had a fort nearby. Mark doubted that. The vine was very old indeed, but he couldn't tell how old. Plus, he doubted the colonists, who had bigger problems, spent their days tending to a grape vine that grew New World local grapes. It was much more likely that the natives grew it, or it was something planted in the 1800s. Mark didn't really care. He liked the story, but right now he needed to get it healthy.

He had already removed some of the dying vine, and had exposed the root, so to get more water into the root system. There really wasn't much he could do except get the plant to drink as much water as possible to dilute the toxins, but it seemed like it was working. He would save the vine, even if the leaves died off this season.

Mark dug into the soil, dry, crumbly and sandy, perfect for grapes, and stuck his hose into the well. As he flushed the root with water, he watched the material around the root float up. Something strange caught his eye. It was a thin shaft of wood with something tied to it. Mark reached in to get it, and the tip scratched him.

"Ow," he made more of a comment on the event than an actual cry of pain. Mark was used to getting poked by thorns and sticks. This was no bit of nature though. Well, not entirely. He pulled it out to discover it was the front half of an arrow, tipped with what looked like a shark tooth.

He took it to the home owner, asking if it was some toy a kid made and left there.

"I can't imagine that it's real. The natives here didn't use shark teeth, did they? For arrowheads? Didn't they make them out of stone like other tribes?"

The owner was impressed with the find, but unsure. "I don't know. It's not a toy. Not mine anyway," he laughed. "You know what? You oughta go see ol' Tommy Blivens. He knows about all this stuff."

The next morning, Mark paid a visit to the local historian, Tommy Blivens, in the old man's back yard. "You know the legend of the White Doe?" asked Tommy.

Mark admitted he never had heard of it. The islands abounded with tales.

"Well, let me tell you." Tommy pointed at the arrowhead. "You might be surprised about your find there...

"Most folks know the main part of the story, how the colonists came over, trying to start the first English colony in the New World. And how Virginia Dare was the first English baby born in the New World. And then there's the Lost Colony, how they went missing in the three years John White was gone.

Now, here's where history and legend start getting confused. History says that the colony just gave up and failed, and the colonists left to Hatteras. But the legend tells something more.

Now, there were two tribes that knew of the colonists, led by the friendly Chief Manteo, and the hateful Chief Wanchese. While Manteo was out fishing for his tribe, Wanchese decided to wipe the settlers out. He attacked the village, setting it on fire, and sending the survivors to their fort, where they fought back against the attacking natives.

Chief Manteo rushed to the aid of the colonists, sneaking them out of the fort through a secret tunnel. He even saved the baby Virginia Dare and her parents.

Safe from the threat within the tribe of Chief Manteo, Virginia grew into a beautiful teenage maiden. She was worshiped because of her unique looks, long blonde hair and blue eyes. She told the stories her parents told, of a world she only knew from their tales, of big cities and canoes that sailed on giant wings. Soon the natives began to come to her for advice and decision, and ultimately to worship her.

Virginia didn't like being considered any more than a young girl, and she implored them not to look at her as a goddess. But she was also patient, shy, and kind to a fault. She always held their council, and always gave the natives heartfelt attention.

This mixture of exotic physical features and her kind heart made Virginia the object of many man's affection, though she never felt the desire to return it. She was far too shy, and would think that picking any one man would be unfair. That never stopped the men of the tribes from admiring her

There was this one Croatan, a young man named Okisko, who had completely fallen for Virginia. Okisko was normally outgoing, fit, dependable, an asset to the tribe, and one of their bravest and strongest men. He could out hunt or out fish or out fight any other young man in the tribe. But when it came to Virginia Dare, he just got weak. He never was able to tell her his feelings, and while Virginia suspected something, she was too shy and polite to mention it.

Now, Okisko certainly wasn't the only man in love with Virginia Dare; there were many who sought her affection. One was an old witch doctor, a shaman, from an inland village. Old Chico had heard of the rare beauty of Virginia, a strange golden haired and blue eyed maiden that was seen to be a goddess by the local Croatan. He had come over the sound to see her during a trading expedition, and he, too, fell in love. But Old Chico had a hard, cold heart. He didn't understand love. He only saw Virginia as a possession. When she spurned his advances, he promised that if she wouldn't be his, she would be no one's.

So he worked his dark magic. Chico gathered magic pearls from mussels, tiny pied or spotted pearls that were the trapped souls of evil water nymphs. Nymphs were incredibly powerful creatures, but when they angered the God of the Waters, they were cursed and frozen into these pearls. Willing to do anything to free themselves, they would promise their magic to whoever let them free.

Chico knew the magic to free them. He whispered his demands to each as he strung them into a necklace, and as each one agreed to his wish, the pearl would glow in an otherworldly luminescence.

The next chance he had, he sailed over to Hatteras to see Virginia. He began by showing her his canoe, promising it to be the fastest on the water, sleek, and quick. He offered her the first trip in it, and being the polite young lady that she was, she meekly accepted. He promised a short trip to the holy grounds along Roanoke Island, her former home.

Old Chico did nothing untoward to her during the trip, trying to make her comfortable on the little craft. They sailed and paddled a little along the soundside shore, taking her up the water near her land, now empty. The old shaman let the canoe slow in the water, with the bow trickling in the lapping waves. Old Chico then presented Virginia with his gift, the pearl necklace.

Being polite, she put the necklace on. It was beautiful, yes, she agreed, incredibly fine and delicate. But in her heart she knew she couldn't keep it. She would have to return it to the old man when they got back home. She would keep in on during the trip, as she was fascinated with how it glows even in the morning light.

Old Chico insisted that she wear it as they approached Roanoke Island, where she had been saved as a baby. Virginia, unsure of her safety but wanting to be off of the canoe with the sly Chico, hopped off the boat and into the sand of her first home.

Now, the water nymphs were powerful creatures, but could not use their wicked magic over the water, as they were at the whims of greater magic. But on land, they were able to act freely. As Virginia took her first steps, she began to change. Her feet went from the dainty pads of a young girl to the soft clops of a deer's hooves. She fell to all fours, Her golden hair grew long and white, like spun silk.

Chico watched as the transformation took place. Within seconds, Virginia Dare had transformed from a human girl to a white doe. The creature he created ran off into the forest. Chico, while not satisfied, felt his evil heart settle. He had done something bad to hurt others, and that made him happy. He paddled back to his inland village, alone.

The natives all began to wonder where Virginia had gone. Chico professed innocence, but Okisko knew better. Tales of a snow white doe that ran through the forests of Roanoke Island spread through the tribe. It was a deer that seemed to have the attention of every other deer on the island, and couldn't be hunted or taken by any arrow. Okisko began to suspect that Chico's magic had something to do with Virginia Dare's disappearance. He had tried to capture the deer, but it always slipped away into the forest. The deer would look back with a forlorn gaze, then turn and scamper silently into the woods.

Sure that Virginia Dare, his unspoken love, had been turned into a doe, Okisko sought out his own magic. He searched inland for any kind shaman to help him in his quest to return Virginia Dare back to him. He found help at the inland meeting point of the tribes, where he met the great shaman Wenaudon, who hated Chico for all the evil the man had spread. Wenaudon was willing to help Okisko, but it would be difficult. Chico, as bad as he was, had very strong magic.

Wenaudon took Okisko into the woods to tell him the secrets that would return Virginia to human form. First, he tasked Okisko to catch and remove a large tooth from a shark and return the shark to the water. Then, Okisko must affix three pearls to the points of the tooth so that it would still cut the curse without hurting the doe. Attach the arrowhead to a straight branch of wood never used for an arrow, using feathers from a heron as the fletching.

Then, Wenaudon told his most important secret. There was a magic spring on Roanoke Island, where the good nymphs gathered to celebrate and dance. They kept the spring enchanted with magic fresh water to preserve its goodness. Okisko had to take the arrow to the spring, leave it there for three days and nights before a full moon while keeping the nymphs away. On the end of the third day, remove the arrow and ask the spirits of the land to allow you to remove the curse.

Okisko returned to his home, tasked with a difficult and long task, but one that he would accomplish for his love.

It took almost a month to do all the steps, and he was singularly devoted, unknowing to any other things that were happening in his world.

So, unbeknownst to him, the son of Wanchese, now the new chief of that tribe, had called for a meeting of the tribes to discuss a peace. Young Wanchese said everyone had tired of the fighting, and they needed to work together. He proposed a group hunt, to finally kill the prized white doe. Secretly, he wanted to kill the doe himself, to use the hunt and the pelt to declare himself chief of all tribes.

He would hunt and kill the elusive white doe with a silver arrow, which was a gift to his father from Queen Elizabeth. If any arrow could find its mark, that one would.

So it was that both Wanchese and Okisko hunted the same creature, to entirely different ends. Okisko looking to return life, while Wanchese wanted to extinguish it.

Both hunted the doe that day. Finally, they both found it, one on the opposite side of the other, unable to see one another through the thick Roanoke forest. Okisko spotted the doe and quickly raised his bow and magic arrow, breathing out silently as he thought a prayer to the spirits to guide his shot. Wanchese did the same, only his thoughts were only of himself. Okisko's arrow flew first, followed within a second later by Wanchese's silver shafted weapon. Okisko saw the arrow strike, but not penetrate the doe, and Virginia Dare was immediately returned to her physical human form. Then Wanchese's arrow struck, cutting through flesh and bone, penetrating her heart.

Wanchese was stunned and in terror at what he had done. He surely thought he shot the white doe, but saw a woman fall. He ran away in fear and cowardice. He had killed someone. He would never be the great leader he wanted with that act.

Okisko ran toward his beloved. He found her on the ground, his arrow next to her, and with a silver arrow in her heart. Virginia Dare had returned and died within the same breath.

Okisko's heart was crushed as well. He had gained his love and lost her within moments.

Saddened, but undaunted, Okisko would not let her die in vain. He grabbed his arrow and ran to the magical sacred spring. His strength carried him only to the waters, no farther, where he collapsed. On his knees, he plunged the arrow into the bubbling water, and asked the spirits for one more deed.

His words were no sooner spoken than the spring began to dry up, collapsing on the arrow. The shaft took root and sprigs of leaves began to grow from the wood. Before Okisko's very eyes a vine grew up and out of the spring. It burgeoned into a canopy, sheltering him from the last heat of the day. Okisko rested under the shade until he had enough strength to return to where he left his beloved.

When he finally made it back to the forest, he found Virginia Dare's body to be gone. There was no sign of her anywhere. The sun was setting and the soft glow of twilight filled the woods with long shadows. Out of the corner of his eye, Okisko saw a flash of white. A small white doe ran, stopped, looked his way, and disappeared into the forest.

Okisko was saddened to lose his beloved Virginia, but happy his wish had been granted. Virginia Dare had been brought back to life, but as the immortal white doe. The doe was seen in the woods, rarely, and never hunted again. The natives all feared the repercussions of even trying to take such a sacred animal."

And with that long tale, while Mark sat rapt at the storytelling of Tommy Blivens, the old historian ended his account. "The white doe has been seen ever since, for hundreds of years, over in the woods near the Lost Colony. No one hunts for it; no one would dare.

"But to your arrow, well, I'm not sayin' it is, I'm not sayin' it ain't, but the legend goes on to say that the vine that grew from the spring turned into Mother Vineyard."

Mark smiled, delighted in the tale. "It's as good a reason as any," he laughed, "Probably better." Mark doubted the arrow he found was Okisko's. It surely would have rotted away by now, he assumed. It would make a good souvenir, he thought, if the homeowners didn't want it.

Mark thanked Mr. Blivens and left to continue his work. Back at the vine, Mark continued his treatment of the plant. It seemed to do well, but he was concerned that the growth was still small, and no insects came to the vine. During the next few days, Mark would half imagine he heard the rustling of an animal in the woods. Turning to look, he hoped to see a white doe, but whatever the creature was, it escaped him.

Mark had little left that he could do to save the plant, so he dug up all the soil around the root and replaced it with rich well draining soil and sand. Then he placed a hose on it just to flood the plant. He hoped he could wash the poison out of the soil that way. He then left for the day.

The next morning, he found the vine looking green and vibrant, probably from all that water and sun. He noticed that the vines were pulled, and some leaves missing, but not fallen. Something had eaten on them. When he got to the trunk of the vine, a twisted base as thick as his body, the ground was still soft, loamy, and wet from the water. The soil had compacted to a smooth surface. But on the top, Mark found the prints of small hooves.

"So that is what's eating my plant."

Joe Sledge

The Last Ghost Of Bodie Island Light

It's not a surprise for a lighthouse to be haunted. They are often on isolated islands, far from any sense of civilization. Keepers, even those with families, would spend most of the time alone. Bodie Island was an island in more than one sense. Alone, in the woods, no real roads to get to even the nearest town of Manteo, the keepers sometimes had to resort to a rowboat to move about. The nearest school had no way of getting kids to and from the keeper's house, so the families had to live somewhere else while the keepers worked diligently, day and night, to keep the light clean and burning.

Even the lighthouse had a tragic history. The first light was built in 1847, but fell over soon after. A replacement light stood for only two years before it, too, was brought down. This time the Civil War claimed it as an early victim when the Confederates destroyed the tower rather than let the invading Union soldiers use it as an observation post. It wasn't until 1872 that the current light was built, far from the shore, alone along the sound and marshes. It was manned by lighthouse keepers until 1940, when the light was fully automated.

Bodie Island doesn't have a real ghost legend attached to it. The one tale always tells of a knocking that occurs every day in the afternoon which comes from behind a sealed up fireplace in the keepers quarters. But there is no legend or tale behind the story. No one has ever heard it happen.

But something much stranger has occurred.

Lauren Gaskill was working at the gift shop in the keepers house selling books and souvenirs to visitors to Bodie Island lighthouse. She knew lots of stories about the light and its history, since she was surrounded by books about the very place she worked. Every day she was able to see the light standing just outside her window. Not much changed except the angle of the sun, but it still was nice to be surrounded by nature and history. The job was fun, and she got to meet plenty of people. Every day she would ring up customers until closing time, then close up, balance the register, and go upstairs to restock before going home in the evening. On winter days the sun would set early and she would stay to see the light come on. In the summer she would linger until twilight, waiting for the beacon to come on.

Then one day, the register started going crazy, ringing up items even as she sat several feet away, and no customers were near the counter. They weren't items that were sold, forgotten to be rung up, piling up in the register's memory. It just starting ringing up prices and spewing out a receipt, longer and longer. It was just weird.

But, well, weird things happen with electronics sometimes. She tried not to think about it.

Closing up, she went upstairs to gather some stock for the next day. Upstairs was empty of people; it was just storage for books and a little bit of things for the Park Service. Rangers came up less often than she did. Tonight they had closed up the counter and locked their doors. Most of the rangers were gone. One would stick around to make sure the evening visitors, mostly photographers, were staying in a safe spot. The ranger would come by later and jiggle the locks, but for now, she was alone in the quarters. Which wasn't really a big deal. She gathered her items and took them back down, closing the door to the dusty upstairs behind her.

Setting down her books and toys, she began organizing and setting out her inventory. As she neatly placed her items, she heard a quiet thump from upstairs. Only half recognizing it, the noise barely registered on her mind. But the second thump, that she noticed.

Stopping with her work, she heard the sounds clearly. Someone was walking around upstairs. The problem was, she knew no one was up there. She was the only one who went up there, and the only one in the whole building. The footsteps got louder, more distinct. It was definitely a big person, an adult. But that was impossible. Then the footsteps stopped walking around, and started heading toward the hallway upstairs.

The hallway led to the upstairs door, she knew.

Which would lead to the stairs.

Which lead to the downstairs, where she was.

The stocking would wait until tomorrow, she thought as she locked the door and hurried to her car. She would come in a little late tomorrow, just to make sure someone else was there. Well, someone else that was supposed to be there.

The next day, Lauren got there in time to finish her work. And she had one of the rangers go upstairs with her. The doors were still locked, and nothing was disturbed. The whole place looked like no one had been up there, except for her occasional visits. Lauren decided that from then on, she wouldn't stock the store without someone else to help. And she won't stay in the keepers house alone.

So who was paying a visit? Well, no one knows. The park service generally frowns upon discussion of ghost stories and investigations, since they aren't a part of the official history, so no one has been able to determine if these things happen often or ever, but Lauren has an idea.

See, Vernon Gaskill, Sr. was the last keeper to tend to the lighthouse. He left in 1940 once the light was automated to head up a buoy tending job, which was much more prestigious and important. Then he retired to spend more time with his family, who would go on to have family of their own. Vernon especially liked his grandchildren, including Lauren.

The Warning Of The Gray Man

Late summer on Hatteras Island was a wonderful time for fishing on the shore. It was still hot and sunny, but the beaches were empty of the families that usually came down during the summer to swelter in the heat of July. Normally the beach would be dotted with tanned children playing in the shore or collecting shells. Dads would stand up tall, formidable, looking over the ocean to spy the rare passing freighter far out to sea. Moms would sit on thin beach towels, resplendent in their black summer shades, enjoying the moment of peace before having to go into someone else's kitchen to cook dinner. But that summer was over. Kids would cram into long station wagons, dad would throw luggage into the big carrier on top, and mom would look wistfully out the window, red lipstick bright on her lips reflecting in the car's side mirror, as she took one last glimpse of the beach for the year.

Now summer was emptying out. The locals came back, reclaiming the beach, with a touch of the hat or a nod to the few visitors left, who were always quieter than the other tourists. It was time to get back to normal. It was time for the locals to get the big surf rods out and go fishing.

Alone on the beach, a man casts his first line of the day. His arms remember the motion, done so often over the years that it becomes second nature. He sees the lure fly far, clearing the rolling waves that crash the shore. A low tide has done nothing to temper the waves, as a hurricane churns offshore somewhere. He has heard on the radio that it will hit farther south. Topsail Island, Beaufort, Atlantic Beach, he doesn't know exactly where. No one does. He knows he has time. Time to cast a line today, maybe tomorrow. Catching something, well, that's a different story. Luck, fate, time, all those things decide where the fish will be when the lure lands. He doesn't care. He reels in and casts again.

Over the sand dune, covered with the thick wavy growth of sea oats and dotted with spiky yucca plants, stands the old beach house. The back porch is shaded, but open to the sea breeze. All the windows are open to take advantage of the natural cooling of the salt air breezes that blew in from the shore. On a rickety table, a transistor radio plays a crackly AM station from farther south with the happy sounds of North Carolina beach swing music. A young lady, the mom, puts up her linens on a white cord across the back of the house. She will have to get them in soon. The summer heat and strong breeze will dry them quickly, but if left too long they will be stiffened and filled with salt air. She knows the storm is coming, but she has time. It's going to hit farther south, says the radio.

Two children play at the end of their sun deck. Mom hears a mix of giggles and complaints, interspersed between the game that the two play, with only the kids knowing the rules. And the rules change depending on the moment. They don't worry about the storm. If there was anything to worry about from a hurricane, their parents would already be doing something about it.

So the kids play. Mom cleans. And Dad fishes, all alone on the shore.

Or not quite alone.

Far down the beach, past the Navy base, past the towering candy striped lighthouse, the land and sea mix together and disappear into a salty haze as the wind blows the waves and air into a mix. Out of this haze walks another man.

He is far away, but then, not that far after all. The fisherman doesn't recognize him as one of the other locals to fish his beach. He knows his neighbors, all the other residents that would come out to his beach. Maybe a tourist, out for a last walk before the showers come?

The man gets nearer and nearer to the fisherman. While he approaches, the fisherman watches him. The strange man is dressed differently than other people who visit the beach. Not in shorts and a shirt, or even regular work clothes, he seems to be in a gray raincoat and Sou'wester, an oilskin rain hat. The fisherman thinks, "That's strange, it's not even raining yet. It won't even be bad enough to put on a hat."

The gray clad man gets closer to the fisherman, who by now has stopped fishing entirely and is staring, waiting for the stranger to get close enough to talk to. Oddly, he still can't make out the face on the visitor.

The man in gray stops, close enough to be seen clearly, but still there are no details to be noticed. He motions to the fisherman, but not a wave of greeting. He waves the man to go in, get away from the waves and shore.

And then the figure vanishes into the salty ether.

And the fisherman realizes who it was. The Gray Man of Hatteras had paid him a visit.

The storm isn't going to hit Topsail, or Atlantic Beach, Beaufort or anywhere else. It is going to come right up the shore to Hatteras, and it will be bad. Someone is going to die.

The father reels in his line and gathers his bucket and tackle. He runs, not walks, back to his house. At the sun deck, he tells his children, "We have to go. Now, The hurricane is turning this way. Go to your mother, we're leaving now."

The two children stop in their tracks for a moment, then run down the walkway to their house. Father throws his tackle haphazardly into storage, his pole into the outdoor shower. Back up on the porch in a flash, he tells his wife, still hanging linen, "We need to leave, the storm's turnin'."

"But, no one's said anything about it on the radio," she wants to protest. She just got the sheets hung, and they haven't dried yet. If they leave, the sheets will blow off in the wind, or at least get dirty and filled with sand.

"We're going, honey, we need to leave, and now."

In the house, the kids run around, closing the windows with a scrape and a thunk. The windows are old, with big shades over them that stick out on hinges, providing shade to the house, but letting the air inside. They are pushed out on long sticks at the bottom, and are wedged in to hold the big shutters out. "Don't worry about the windows, kids, we need to leave now!" One more scrape and thump meant the last upstairs window closed, but the few downstairs remain open. The inside of the house would be soaked if the rains came hard.

He hurries through the house, finding just enough time to gather clothes for a few nights. Mother and father rush the kids out the door to their car. It will be a long drive to get to the mainland. A stop and wait at Oregon Inlet to take the ferry over to Bodie Island would prolong the wait. They would hope that most of the tourists' cars have already left, and that the wait will be short.

The rain would catch up with the family as they drove inland. Spatters of raindrops pelted the windshield in big pats. The sky became overcast and gloomy. The hurricane would bring up the thick aroma of the tropics along with cold rain, making it a dismal trip. The family found a motel inland, just far enough to avoid the onslaught of wind and rain. On the motel TV they would receive sporadic reports of what was happening, but they wouldn't know for sure until the next day. The kids had fun, jumping on the beds, running to and from the ice machine, and generally staring out the motel room's window at the changing weather. They would all finally fall into a fitful sleep, wondering what tomorrow would bring.

It would be two days until the family could get back to their home on Hatteras Island. The roads were covered with sand, and the ferry would have difficulty crossing the notoriously changeable Oregon Inlet. The mother worried at what she would find; her laundry was the least of her worries. They heard of all the damage on the radio. Eight people died along the coast, and over a hundred were injured. Houses were damaged or destroyed. They passed places they barely recognized from all the storm damage.

But when the family got home, their house still stood. Even the shutters still hung from the windows. Going inside, the house was untouched. No rain entered the windows, no sand had blown in from the storm, even the linen still hung loosely from the clothesline. The house had been protected by the Gray Man of Hatteras.

The father had known of the legend of the Gray Man, but he never thought he would see the apparition firsthand. No one knew who it was. Some thought he was a sailor who was lost at sea during a hurricane long ago, before there was any chance of predicting the storms. Others speculated he was a force of weather itself, where the storm formed a spirit to warn people of the impending threat. It was always the same story...

A ghostly figure, clad all in gray, no distinguishing features to describe him, appears to someone along the Hatteras coast. It is not a malevolent spirit. It appears more pleading, a silent gesture to get off the beach. There is an unspoken communication that is understood, and that is to leave, immediately. Do not wait, the storm is coming to Hatteras. And it will be a particularly dangerous one.

But if the people that see the Gray Man heed his wordless warning, he will invoke protection upon their home. People who have seen the Gray Man describe coming back to their home the same way this family did. Sometimes there is nothing but sand blown around the house, other times, the house is immaculate. No windows are broken, no rain has come in. The house, and its inhabitants, are protected.

Ghosts At The Light

I had joined a ghost hunting team to go investigate all the local legends around Hatteras Island early one summer. Being a local, at least regionally, as I was from Kitty Hawk, they thought I would have a proper sense of history, and "know where to look." Being a historian and a surfer helped immensely. But all my studies didn't prepare me for the tales and legends I would find. Or what happened when we were done.

The plan was elegant, and I had great respect for the people that planned this out. This was no mere

73

ghost hunt, stalking with nets and laser beams, or whatever they used. My job was to go first, alone, and find all the legends, document them, but keep them secret. I spent a lot more time at the local libraries and bookstores than I did in any haunted house, I'll tell you.

When I found the beginnings of the tales, I went to where they were supposed to happen, just to get a feel for the stories. If there were supposed to be spooks rising from an old graveyard on the sound, well, there better be a graveyard there.

So, I took my notes, made comparisons, found the legends, what was behind the legends, and the variations. It was pretty full of stories, let me tell you. Here are some of what I found.

To start with, I'll mention the ghost ship of Hatteras, the *Carroll A. Deering*. It's probably the most famous shipwreck around these parts, except for maybe the *Monitor*. The *Deering* was found on a winter morning, stranded and floundering in a cold sea. Oddly, the *Deering* was remarkably shipshape for an abandoned craft. Its sails were tied or set, it was perfectly seaworthy, but no one, not a soul was on it. The mess was even set for a meal. It was more like the crew and passengers just vanished. They never turned up in lifeboats, never were found at sea. The only witness to the events on board was a lucky six toed cat, a mouser kept on the ship to keep the rodent population down. The poor cat was brought to land, and seemed to have become a prodigious breeder, with six toed cats wandering the island now, some even becoming pets for the lighthouse keepers.

I only tell this story briefly, mostly because it really has no ghostly overtones, and partly because it will come back to haunt me later. The *Deering* is more a ghost ship in that it was abandoned, much like a ghost town. There are no haunts from it.

Other tales are more appropriate.

The nickname for the coast is The Graveyard of the Atlantic, and the name truly fits. It was named so because of all the ships that went down in the turbulent waters, where currents meet and cross, or shallow sandbars reach up to grab unsuspecting sailing ships, stopping them in a shuddering grasp, breaking the hulls and shattering the masts. Less well known, I discovered, but possibly more appropriate, were the tales of the unknown dead that have littered the shore.

Since it was impossible to determine the name of a person, just who they were to tell the next of kin, any bodies found on the shore from a shipwreck were often buried near where they were found. The salt and sun would quickly take their toll on a body. So the natives hurriedly buried any remains before they began to rot, which sometimes meant the bodies were simply buried in the sand near where they were found.

Legends tell that when the wind blows from offshore, the skeletal remains become uncovered. And when the skeletons become uncovered, the ghosts walk the land. I found several "first hand" tales of ghosts appearing near the light, or walking by the highway, after storms, and corresponding skeletons turning up on the beach. When the bones were either reburied, or removed and given a more proper burial, the ghosts stopped appearing.

A ghost of a young lady, clad all in gray, is often seen when her grave is uncovered at a nearby cemetery. She will be seen crossing the road nearby, only to vanish if anyone gets close. Once the graves are cared for, she stops her spectral walks.

I was never able to determine who the young woman was, even after a visit to the cemetery. Her name and her life remained as much a mystery as her afterlife. Still, it was something.

Even spookier still were the tales of the shadow people. This was a similar tale to the ghost lady, but just vaguely different enough that I separated it into a different file. These were told to me to be truly shadow figures, black, not even gray, but transparent. "Like smoke?" I asked an old local. "Naw," he declared in his twangy Outer Banks brogue. "It's more like a shadow, but standin' up." His description was both simple, and quite frightening. A walking shadow. And there seemed to be lots of them, twenty, forty, sixty, I never got one answer. They just always appeared at twilight, as the sun sets, walking around the base of the lighthouse. The big light stood only a few hundred feet from the ocean, and may have even been a makeshift grave marker for many of the dead, though I can't imagine burying bodies at the foot of the light.

Still, the tale did cool my blood and shiver my skin some. The group of shadow people walk up the beach in a long, slow ragged line, all looking like they just survived a shipwreck. They plod toward the low dunes to an open spot where the lighthouse sits, and slowly vanish into the dark.

Some people have even said that they enter the locked metal doors of the light, and climb the stairs. I imagined a macabre conga line of shadows going up and up to the light, only to vanish into the brick ether.

There was no time of year for the event, no anniversary to it, no normal occurrence that I could go and visit, which was disappointing. Some tied it to the

Deering, but pretty much most of the legends make it out to be something different. That one would also be difficult to investigate. We may have to just wait, camp out every evening to see if we ever saw the event, which seemed difficult and unlikely.

The next legend I found seemed more promising. A ghost haunted the big Cape Hatteras Lighthouse, and the beach nearby. An apparition has been seen wearing the rain gear of a sailor or surfman both in the light and on the shore. He also appears in the evening, but a lot of locals swear they have seen him. He appears so often that he has been given the nickname Bob, though that being the actual name is likely apocryphal. The figure seems to have ties to the light, possibly a keeper or assistant. I found little in history to attach one specific keeper to the light. There were no deaths, no unfinished business, and no Bob. That didn't mean he didn't exist; it's just that his story had yet to be discovered, which I appreciated as a challenge. We very well may see Bob, or get a recording of him.

I had gathered my information, all the places to visit, and awaited the arrival of the other members. One of them was an empath, or psychic. I had dealt with the vagaries of perceptives in the past, usually not in a group, and found them to be lacking, severely. I often got only weird obfuscation, some general statements that could go any way, like going to a graveyard and them saying "There is death here." I found a few spots that had absolutely no legend attached to them and planned to go to them, merely as a baseline. I even asked about some old houses to the locals.

The meeting place, well, one of many on the long thin island, was the Red & White grocery store, a true

landmark that sent people either south to the ferry docks
or west to the marina. It was the place to stock up for the
day or week. I had visited to get a sandwich, when one of
the workers told me one last legend, that I, mostly,
believed.

She had pointed out the numerous feral cats that
wandered the parking lot, living in the nearby bushes.
They awaited a moment of quiet until they snuck out to
raid the dumpster or eat from a community table of sorts,
as the lady at the store fed the wild furballs. I had seen
them before, and admired them (I was and am very much
a cat person, loving their quiet aloofness. If not for their
fear of water, they would make excellent surfers.) I left
them be, wild as they were, to do their thing without any
help on my part, but she explained their origin.

"You see," she started, "They all came from one
daddy cat. That one that came off of the *Deering* when it
got sunk out there. When the Coast Guard went on board,
all they found was this big fat cat with six toes. So they
brought him ashore, had to save someone, I guess, and he
started makin' babies, and it just took off from there."

She walked out with me, taking a small bag of food.
"They know me," she stated. "Heeeerrrre, kittykittykitty!"
she called and the creatures came running. She spread
some food, treats, some sort of goodies out and the cats
ate with a stoic voraciousness. One cat, a big black and
white tom, must have sensed my admiration and began to
rub my leg. She bent down to pick up the cat, taking his
huge paw in her fingers and lightly squeezing. "See?" she
asked, "See how he's got six toes?"

The cat twisted and scrambled from her arm, and she
let him tumble to the rest of the kitties, licking himself

clean for good measure. I knew the cats would scamper if I tried to pick them up.

"You know," she told me conspiratorially, "One of these cats haunts the lighthouse."

I assumed she was teasing, knowing how I was researching legends. I smiled and thanked her for telling me about the cats, and the legend, and showing me the paws.

So, the rest of the investigators showed up the next day, and we met to send everyone to their tasks. I gave the locations of various places, the graveyard in Buxton, the old Cora Tree, and of course the lighthouse and beach. I included the location of the old lighthouse, with barely a few remains still lingering on the shore where the original light had been demolished over a century ago.

I was impressed at the results we got, even when we got no results. A storm had recently blown in and the graves in Buxton were well covered. We didn't have any luck with spotting a woman ghost wandering the roads late at night, nor did we find any of the spectral signals that often emanate from a haunted spot. The ghosts, if there were any, seemed to be well at rest.

There was little luck on the beach near the lighthouse. We waited into the dark, taking video and photos, while the audio recordings didn't do very well with the evening breeze and Hatteras' notorious waves. A few grim shimmers on the 8mm tapes gave some of the ghost hunters a glimmer of hope, but nothing compared to the tales of troupes of spectral shadows wandering the shore up to the now flashing lighthouse.

I began to feel a little bit of what the ghost hunters must have felt while we were out there. As much as I was used to the area, it was close enough to home that I had come to these waves often enough to see them wash near to the base of the light on several occasions. I knew the intimacy of the stories. I felt like I knew who these people were that we looked for. Not their names or faces, but who they were. Lonely, lost, or gone too soon, I could see how someone could haunt this land. I was almost disappointed that we didn't see anything.

The next day we toured the area where the old lighthouse had stood. It was torn down after the Civil War and just left to rubble. I had sat on the old sandstone blocks as a kid. A storm had blown in about six years ago and washed the dune away, taking the remains of the lighthouse with it. It was mostly to kill time until we could investigate the new lighthouse.

By then it was evening, and most of the tourists were done with their visits. The parking lot was emptying out, and even the cars with surfboard racks were driving away, as the ocean had turned a devious calm. The sun began its dip toward Trent Woods, a wholly mysterious place that I was surprised held no legends. It was long the home of indigenous tribes, the true locals of the land, and must have had some secrets. Unfortunately, they were not told to me.

One of the park rangers had met with me earlier in the week. Professing both my love of the coast, and my local credibility as well as my historical background, and a little bit of harmless charm, I had persuaded him to open the doors to the light, just to see some of the insides which were generally hidden from public. He happily acquiesced even after learning I was part of a paranormal group, and would be showing the insides of Cape Hatteras Light to a bunch of "ghostbusters." He jokingly asked, "Which one of you is Kong?"

We weren't really sure if he would let us do more than a couple photos and some video of the entrance, but he seemed delighted in watching the setup and seeing the gear. We couldn't go up the stairs, the metal rails were far too narrow and rickety, but we were welcome to stay inside.

The room got hot and quiet, with only the *click* of the camera and a bit of whir from the 8mm video cam. The light got dark quickly without the bright sunlight pouring through the small windows on the sides. Finally, one of the team got out the recorder and began asking questions, seeing if we could persuade "Bob" to talk.

She asked if anyone was there, if they could give us a sign, to move something or make a noise. We all waited. Honestly, the feeling made my skin crawl a little, but I almost hoped something would happen. It would have been nice to at least give Bob, or whoever he was, a bit of permanence, just take him out of legend. The team member asking the questions looked at their empath, who gave a shaky wave of his hand, then whispered, "Go on, ... maybe... someone's listening."

I couldn't tell if he meant that it couldn't hurt, or if he just wasn't sure yet.

It may have been my imagination, it could have just been the wind, even though we were inside on a hot evening, but we all kept feeling like something was there. It just got colder, the air, well, it didn't stir, it just...moved.

And then everything went back to normal.

We decided immediately that the inside of the light was getting a little crowded, so everyone left and went outside into the now orange light of a late day.

"Did everyone feel that?" asked our empath.

"Does that happen often?" the park ranger inquired. He was slightly ashen. They were used to real history, tangible stuff. Getting the heebee geebees wasn't part of the job.

"Yeah… and no," answered our lead investigator. It was a cryptic but oddly accurate response.

We gathered by the keeper's quarters to see if we got anything, but the video and audio didn't give us much. The team would have to meet in a quieter room with time to look over a TV screen to really tell. We all decided to meet up for dinner and go to the motel and check what we found that night. We invited the ranger to come by, but he politely declined. I was not surprised.

As we left for the parking lot, I said I was going to stick around a little longer, just to go watch the waves come in. The rest bid their goodbyes, and I wandered back to the light and the beach.

The waves still rolled in over the jetties but there was no heart in them now. Evening was a time of rest, even for the ocean. I strolled back, in no hurry, to my car.

Wandering around the light, the beacon came on, the bright white aerobeacon hunting for ships at sea. I spied one of the feral cats, like I had seen at the Red & White. No fear in its green eyes, the big black and white tom came prowling up to me. It wasn't the same one I had seen earlier, no doubt, but it could be a close relative. This fat fellow certainly did his part to keep the mouse population down on the island. It walked up to me, purring and chittering a happy song. It turned its body sideways to rub my legs, walking with a purpose as he intertwined himself in my shins.

Like I said, I am at heart a cat person. I leaned down to pick up the friendly tom and give him a scratch on the ears.

And he vanished in my hands like a puff of smoke.

I can say only this, I certainly had a good story to tell at dinner that night.

Joe Sledge

The Cora Tree

"You stay well away from that Cora woman and her knee-baby," James Farrow would admonish his children, and any others, whenever they passed the strange woman and her child along the sandy paths that crossed through the twisted yaupon and live oak that covered the west of Cape Hatteras. "You don't go messin' with her. You give her some respect."

Respect. More like fear. Farrow knew all too well what everyone else knew, but never said to Cora's face, or within earshot. Cora was a witch.

The families that dotted the coast and sound of Cape Hatteras in the 1700s could ill afford a bad day from the spooky woman. A few of the families had cows that provided much needed milk to the children and the hard working adults. So when a man didn't seem to treat Cora with the deference she preferred, coming near her and her child as they passed on one of the sand paths, Cora drug her finger across the cow's side. From that day forward, the cow never gave a drop of milk.

When a rambunctious boy gave a sneer at the little toddler always at Cora's side, a strange child who never laughed nor cried, but stared with a strange intensity at everything and everyone, the boy came down with a severe fever. He lay in bed on fire, burning from within for days, until a gold coin was placed upon Cora's doorstep one morning. The fever vanished as quickly as it set in.

So, while the people of Hatteras had no proof of Cora being a witch, they all knew. They all kept away from her, and kept their kids close when she was nearby.

Now, James Farrow was a local sailing captain. He would go out almost every day to catch fish, and he was successful in his work, most of the time. What people didn't know was that on some days, when the wind was blowing up, or the sky turned red in the morning, as he prepared to sail out, he would often row over to Cora's pier, when she wasn't out, and leave a penny on the dock near her little shack in the reeds. Some fishermen would come back empty, some with a few fish, but Captain Farrow always came back just a little luckier than the others. Even if it just was having a safer trip when the Cape blew up a storm.

Now, Captain Farrow was known for his fairness, and he was well respected in the village. He was the person everyone looked to when there was a problem, and they listened to him even when he said there wasn't a solution. If James Farrow didn't know what to do, well, there was nothing to do.

Sometimes shipwrecks occurred off the coast, washing up strange items from the Caribbean that were meant for the big ports up north in Boston or New York. The islanders would scavenge what they could, all the way to using the wood from ships to build their houses and the flags to make their blankets. Less often there would be the survivors of these shipwrecks, sailors and officers from far away, different in their languages and beliefs, and their attitudes.

So it was one summer day that a ship, skirting close to the coast to pick up the fast moving northward water, found itself too close to the oft changing shoals of the cape. It ran aground and cracked itself open, spilling its valuable contents from the exotic tropics out onto the shallows. No one was injured, and the crew, a loose band of freed slaves from the Caribbean led by their fiery Captain, Eli Blood, hauled their valuable cargo to the shore, where they quickly set up a raucous camp under the sails of their stricken ship.

The locals, somewhat aghast at the wild shenanigans of the crew as they watched the sailors drink and dance into the night, came to render what help they could. The crew would stay upon the sun-kissed beach, happy to be on the mild summer shores without a care until a ship could be sent from Massachusetts to recover the goods and the men. The captain however was required by title to have more hospitable accommodations, and Captain Farrow offered to put him up in Farrow's modest but sincere cottage. Captain Blood a rough blooded northerner, harsh in language and quick in temper, well suited for the difficult life at sea, where orders had to be obeyed and time was precious. He found himself ill fitted for the patient life of a fisherman, but did his best to be respectful of his host and the village that welcomed him.

The only thing he couldn't stand was the talk of Cora, "the witch." Blood shook his head, grumbled, and cursed every time her name was brought up, or when she passed by and the islanders paid her reverence.

"Why, this would never do!" he blustered, too loud, and too often. The locals would quietly wish him to shush, to mind himself. They didn't want to be on the bad end of one of Cora's curses. But Blood paid no mind, and he stewed in his judgement.

So when a local boy, well liked and a scion of a good family, was found dead on the shore, the New England skipper had had enough of just talk. The boy was found with a frozen rictus of pure terror upon his face, and a mark burned into his forehead as if by a finger aflame, 666, the mark of the beast. Captain Blood could perceive only one perpetrator, the one that left small dainty footprints away from the body. Small, like a woman's.

He knew it had to be Cora.

So he gathered his crew, steeled themselves with spirits mixed with verses from the Bible, and went after the woman and her baby, alone in her shack in the reeds.

The mob gathered her up and took her to the village. Captain Blood proclaimed himself a witch hunter, having been from Massachusetts, home of the Salem Witch Trials. He knew how to test to see if Cora truly was a witch.

Captain Farrow and the locals where terrified. Most refused to speak or acknowledge the charge, but were also unable to look away. Farrow begged the charged and angered Captain Blood to rethink his actions. He pleaded,

"I know it seems bad, but we must wait! We can take her to a court, let us judge her fairly!" His pleas fell upon deaf ears. Blood and his compatriots shoved Captain Farrow aside.

"I know how to deal with these witches!" he bragged.

First, Blood bound Cora hand and foot, then announced he would throw her into the water. A witch would use her powers to save herself and float, while a mortal would sink. He then had his crew toss her into the shallows of the sound, to have her thrash as she tried to turn and free herself. Her head above water, Blood saw the first trial completed in his favor.

Next, he drew his knife. He gathered her hair into a clump, pulling her out of the water. Hacking at the hair, it was thick and wet. He declared it like wire, unable to cut. The second trial again was successful for the hunter, not for the witch, Blood decreed.

Finally, he used his knife to cut Cora's finger, and his own. He let the drops of blood mingle into a bucket, filled with water, and Blood looked into the sanguine liquid. He and his crew all looked, seeing the same thing. Cora was seen in the divination to be cavorting and plotting with the devil himself. All the signs said so, Cora was a witch.

The villagers were more terrified of the drunken stirred up sailors than of Cora by now, and all stood back while the crew dragged Cora to the middle of the village. They took her, along with her knee-baby, and tied both tight to a large tree, then began surrounding the tree with kindling and dried grass.

Again, Captain Farrow pleaded his case. "She may be guilty, but this is not how to do these things. We must follow the law. We do not take another life without proper reason!"

But Captain Blood had already hardened his heart. He wanted to kill and no man would stop him from getting his bounty. He approached the tied Cora, her toddler clinging to her, still no expression on his face.

As Blood got closer, the baby began to change. Soon, he turned, changed shape, and began to grow fur and claws. He became a ferocious hissing cat, spitting and screaming at the approaching Captain Blood and his torch.

By now all the village was in shock, and even the crew began to fear for their lives. But Blood was made of stronger stuff, he told himself. "You will fear me," he insisted, as he approached. As he stepped forward, the sky turned from blue to gray. Clouds rolled in, a heavenly ash, and the air got cold. Wind whipped, villagers screamed and prayed.

Blood was hardened against anything except his task. He stood at the kindling, his torch sputtering. He lowered his hand to touch it to the twigs.

Just then, a tremendous crackle of lightning ripped out of the sky. It crashed into the tree, splitting it in two right to the trunk, just above where Cora and the now ferocious cat were tied. Everyone around the tree were knocked flat, unconscious. Captain Blood was thrown back from the tree, his body battered.

When the village folk awoke, the smell of brimstone was heavy in the air. The tree smoldered, its leaves dried and ashy. The interior of the tree was hollowed and burned. Around the base, the ropes were still tied tight, not an inch of give in them.

Only, Cora was no longer there. She and her child, the baby turned into her familiar, a witch's cat, were gone. She had just vanished into thin air.

Captain Blood awoke last. Stunned, chagrined at his failure, and somewhat embarrassed, he would leave the village and await his rescue for the remainder of the month on the shore with his crew. No word was ever heard from him again.

The villagers were no more fortunate. For the month that Blood remained on the island, fishing was poor. Storms came up quickly, without warning. Nets came up empty, even as fish swam nearby. Captain Farrow even tried leaving a penny on Cora's dock. It sat there every day until the dock fell in from disrepair and rot.

Cora was never seen again. Some think that her cat haunts the woods of the mainland nearby, a ferocious beast that hunts the animals and livestock of the towns. But Cora was gone.

However, she did not leave without making her mark. To this day, the tree still grows. It is split down the middle, looking like two trees from ten feet up, but a single large trunk from the bottom. And in the tree, as if carved with a thin fiery finger, are the letters CORA.

Joe Sledge

The Flaming Ship Of Ocracoke

With the end of summer near, the locals to the Outer Banks often turn their longing and wistful eyes toward the more peaceful times with the coming of Autumn. The water would still be warm, but the beaches would be empty of the usual circus of tourist season. Often this was when the residents would plan their trips to enjoy their coast, that one last time before the weather turned cool.

It was that first trip that Kelly Twiford planned for himself. Newly seventeen, and with a new car, he searched for places close by, but not too close, to go. He was reading old travel books, looking for things to do and places to stay. Just an overnight down to Hatteras was all he wanted. A night or two away, in a campground or little motel, he didn't care, just something fun and different. School was starting and he wanted to have an escape.

He read an old book his parents had on their shelf, discovering some old stories of his home. Living in Nags Head, he didn't always know all the tales from Hatteras and further south. He read one story, just a little paragraph, called *The Flaming Ship of Ocracoke*. There really wasn't much to it, just a spooky tale of a ship that appeared, on fire, the first full moon of the fall.

Kelly looked at his calendar. The first full moon was in the middle of September. On a weekend. On his birthday.

"Well, that settles that," he decided to himself.

A few weeks later, Kelly set off on a Friday afternoon, waving to his parents from his early birthday present, his slightly used car, as he drove down to Hatteras to camp under the light, then the next morning to go into Ocracoke, camp there, and hike out to the beach that evening.

The first night passed uneventfully. Whatever ghosts lingered around the big candy cane lighthouse certainly weren't coming all the way out to see him in his tent. The big light beamed its way over a bright sky when the moon came out clear over the water. The night came on sooner than it had in the summer. Kelly read by candle light and then curled up in his sleeping bag to rest.

The morning brought a still heat to the tent, which led Kelly to packing up quickly. He had little to take in the first place. He got in line to catch the ferry to Ocracoke, talking with families and girls on the ferry while their dads made the mistake of feeding the seagulls.

The little village of Ocracoke was far enough south that the water was noticeably warmer, as was the air. He swam and sweated, showered, hiked the old stomping grounds of Blackbeard, where he supposedly still walked as a ghost, even after losing his head to Maynard. Kelly found the old well out on Springer's Point, but saw no signs of the infamous pirate.

Evening came on early again, and Kelly ate a quiet dinner from the local sandwich shop. He went to his tent, gathered his things, and went out to the soft white sand beach of Ocracoke Island.

Kelly had found the rest of the story of the flaming ship of Ocracoke, but decided to read it on the beach as the sun set and the sky darkened. It was indeed a darker tale than he imagined.

Long ago in the middle of Europe, a group of Palatines, German emigrants who suffered under constant invasion of their lands, had left their war torn region to escape to a more peaceful land. They had hoped to settle with some of their Swiss brethren in the colony of New Bern. Hiring a ship and crew, the refugees packed all their belongings as well as their hidden wealth, and dressed in rags for the trip. It would be long, arduous, and dirty. They had no need for fineries on board, and hid their valuables well.

Unfortunately, one of the crew overheard some of the Palatines discussing their treasure and how they were going to spend it once they arrived in the New World. The captain and crew, disreputable pirates, decided to rob the Palatines on the next night when they arrived in Ocracoke.

So the next day, when they finally spotted land, the ship waved off the small boats that would come alongside to transfer the passengers and their supplies to the shallow bottom boats that could more easily ply the waters around the sound, and take the passengers the rest of the way up to New Bern. The local O'cockers were surprised, but did not press the matter. The crew told the Palatines that they would have to wait one more night on board until they could leave. Surprised, but with no choice, the refugees acquiesced.

That night, as the Palatines slept, the crew snuck into the berths and slaughtered every man, woman, and child in their sleep. They then soaked the ship in oil while loading anything of value into the two row boats on board. They lit the ship on fire, assured in their getaway and the riches to buy anything they desired.

The pirates planned to row in, claiming they barely escaped with their lives, while the ship burned just offshore. With the Palatines already dead, their bodies burned, and the ship sunk, no one would ever know the truth.

But as they began to row to shore, they found the ship to be unconsumed by the fire. It burned, lit up from the flames, but did not collapse from the heat and combustion. Then the pirates heard the wails of the dead. The Palatines, though they were dead with their throats cut in the hold, cried out, a terrifying clamor that became an all encompassing shriek. The boat, far from being overtaken by the fire, seemed to come to life in its conflagration. It began to move, driven by an unseen wind. It sailed toward the panicked pirates. They began to row maniacally, but the row boats were overladen with the ill gotten treasure, and responded poorly to the strain of the oars.

The ship got closer and closer, chasing down the pirates. It rammed into the little boats, splitting them in half, spilling pirate and plunder into the shallow seas. The pirates struggled to stay afloat in the churning waves, but they had filled their pockets with ill gotten gold, and their wet clothes weighted down with treasure held them under the water as they drowned in an uncaring sea.

Some tried to dive into the water, to swim away. They were crushed under the keel of the barnacle encrusted ship.

By this time the few Ocracokers had come out to see the horrible sight. They waited to see if anyone would survive this otherworldly onslaught. The little rowboats sank, weighted down by the treasure. Only broken and splintered remains washed ashore.

The flaming ship, its work now done, turned to head south, then caught the wind, its sails unfurled, flaming and glowing but not consumed, and turned northward. It sailed out to sea and disappeared into the inky night.

Only two men were able to make it to shore. Waterlogged, exhausted, and terrified, they confessed their actions before passing away in front of a small crowd of shocked islanders. No one could believe what the pirates had said, yet they had all just seen it.

Thus the legend of the flaming ship of Ocracoke was born.

Kelly sighed reading the story. It was more horrific than he thought it would be, sad and tragic at the loss of life so close to a new home. The night had come on strong now, and he noticed that his small candle lantern glowed only fitfully in a small circle around him. He let his eyes adjust to the darkness as he blew the lamp out.

Kelly expected the night to engulf him, but strangely, the beach and sky slowly began to come alive around him. Stars appeared, tiny bits of plankton radiated green and blue phosphorescence in the sand and water. And a strange glow appeared over the horizon. Orange light boiled in the water. Kelly saw a diffuse shape take form, a strange low and long pointed shaft began moving away from the barrier of sea and sky. Masts rolled up to the stars, with sparking embers shooting off, only to be fanned as huge sails filled the air, filling in an otherworldly freshening breeze. Kelly saw it, just as the O'Cockers had seen it long ago. The Flaming Ship of Ocracoke had returned.

Kelly stood up, slowly, afraid to break the magic. He didn't know what to do, wave them down, tell them to finally come ashore, or go get help. He was transfixed as the ship came nearer and nearer, turning its bow southward, as if heading toward the inlet south of Ocracoke. The ship continued to burn, but never lost a piece of rigging or a bit of hull. Even the sails filled as if soaked with kerosene but they would not fall to ash like they should. The ship continued its southerly path.

Alone on the beach, Kelly finally sprang into action. It could be a ghost ship, or it could be a real ship in trouble. Either way, someone needed to see it. He ran up the dune, up the road, to find anyone. Finally running into a sheriff's deputy, he called to the man. "There's a ship on fire out there!"

The deputy drove his truck to the access, Kelly close behind. "Now, this isn't some joke is it, kid? This isn't about that ghost ship thing, right?"

A small group had heard Kelly tell his story and had come out. They all walked over to the other side of the dune. The only thing they saw was the low rising moon, clear of the horizon, having just cut through the green fog offshore.

Kelly looked north and south, but nothing disturbed the calm waters of the Atlantic Ocean. He stared. "I'm sure I saw it!" he proclaimed.

"Mebbe it was just the moon coming up," one of the locals suggested, hoping to ease the poor kid's mind and embarrassment a little.

Kelly shook his head. Out of the corner of his eye, he thought he saw something disappear into the lights far to the north.

The rest of the people just shook their heads, happy to have one more story to tell.

Then the wind blew, and a soft wail of anguish came with it.

Joe Sledge

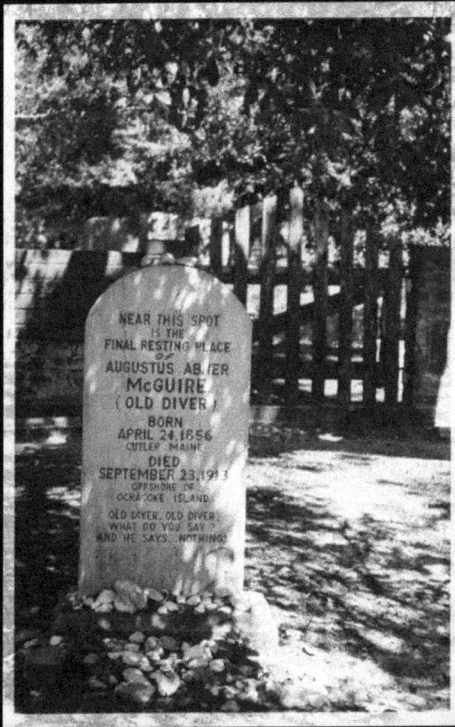

Too Many Ghosts

The blessings of Ocracoke are the pristine beaches, natural landscape, and a true step back in time village that is home to a few hundred residents, of whom many can call pirates their ancestors. But the island has come with a curse, of sorts. The little village, with no easy way on or off, usually means that people on the island stay on, even after death.

Yes, life and death are close acquaintances on the island of Ocracoke. Residents, whether permanent or temporary, as well as those just washed up on the soft sandy shore, will find themselves staying on even after their passing. It's just been that way. With no ability to preserve or return the deceased, a sad death or an expected passing both end up with a quick burial. It's difficult to walk down a road in the evening without passing a spectral guest or resident. You can't even stay in the hotel without meeting one.

The historic Island Inn, once a schoolhouse and lodge, now a cozy hotel, is haunted by a ghost so well known she goes by the name Mrs. Godfrey. The usually invisible lady sits on the edge of the bed at night, holds guests by the ankle, and likes to go through women's make up bags.

Instead, if visitors go for a hike through Springer's Point, they may run into a bearded man who angrily chases them through the thick woods. You'd be angry, too, if you had your head cut off. Blackbeard is said to haunt the woods, as well as seen as a ball of light on the nearby beach.

So, perhaps a walk on the beach? Well, be careful where you step, as many a lost sailor got buried in the sand, their corpses lost to time, but their spirits still rise up to follow beach goers late in the evening.

No visit to Ocracoke is complete without a visit to the lighthouse. There one might see a lady on her way to party, dressed fancy in a long gown. Or even meet the keeper of the light, dressed in his uniform of black and white stripes. Only, there is no keeper for Ocracoke light anymore.

Certainly visitors would expect the graveyard in Ocracoke to be haunted, and prefer to steer clear of that area. Which would be difficult, as there are over eighty of them throughout the village. People were buried where ever there was a spot available. They just don't stay put.

One of the restless guests is Mad Mag, born Margaret Eaton, in Rockland, Maine. At fifteen, the young girl was possibly kidnapped and certainly married to John Simon Howard, who was the captain of a sailing craft at the time, as well as twenty years her senior. He brought her back to Ocracoke, where she remained, developing her character of being a rather crazy mad person. Who can blame her? When her husband died, she moved into a small shack along one of the sandy roads of Ocracoke, where she cursed the local children on a daily basis for banging on the side of her house. She was often seen standing alone and silent in one of the family graveyards that dotted the land. After her death, locals would still spot her, a woman with long white hair, in a gown, standing in the corner of the George Howard cemetery.

While all of the legends have a certain oddity, and a bit of terror to them, there is one that just by the sheer appearance must be the most terrifying of them all. The legend of Old Diver is certainly strange, and his haunting is so scary it kept people inside at night.

Now, Old Diver isn't his real name. It was Augustus Abner McGuire. He was a diver who did repair work on ships, wearing the heavy brass hat diving helmet and weighted boots to keep him underwater. On September 23, 1913, he went down to repair damage on the ship he served upon. It was quickly observed that all was not well, and Augustus was brought back aboard, where he passed away on deck.

His body was brought to nearby Ocracoke where the local keeper of the lifesaving station, David Williams, found a burial plot near his family cemetery. After a quick burial, Augustus' iron weighted boots were placed at a cedar grave marker, and Augustus joined the family of permanent Ocracoke residents.

No one really knew the man, being from somewhere else and never taking a breath on Ocracoke Island, so to the native kids he simply became Old Diver. The children of Ocracoke, no strangers to death and ghosts, began a macabre game, where they would hide behind the gravestones, awaiting a young victim. When a suitably nervous little kid would come by, especially in the twilight, a local girl or boy would call out, "Old Diver, Old Diver, what do you say?" And the kids would await an answer that would never come, so after a very uncomfortable pause, a voice would come from somewhere, hidden but close…
"Nothing."

The game might have been fun for kids to scare one another, but soon enough, the local adults were more than sure that Old Diver actually haunted the sand road that would later become the final home to the British sailors who were victims of the *HMT Bedfordshire* sinking. In the evening, Old Diver, his ghost, would walk the road, fully in his garb of his diving suit, complete with brass helmet, thick canvas jumpsuit, and heavy clomping boots. To see him slowly but silently as the game the kids played implied, walking down the road at night, his body aglow with an unearthly halo, would send locals in terror to their homes, where they would close and lock their doors in hopes of keeping out the otherworldly figure of Old Diver, Augustus Abner McGuire.

His wooden marker rotted away, and his boots were removed to the local museum. A new marker, more visible and better inscribed, sits in between the family cemetery and the British cemetery, but no one knows exactly where Old Diver is truly buried. Some still wonder if he's even in the ground at all.

Joe Sledge

Blackbeard's Final Swim

The five college students drove off the ferry from Hatteras early in the morning to beat the rush of tourists that would crowd the boat later that summer day. Friends from different places were brought together in search of adventure, and the group had found their fun by hang gliding, parasailing, riding jet skis, sailing catamarans, and surfing the big waves of Cape Hatteras. This was the end of the trip for them, a relatively easy day kayaking the shallow waters of Ocracoke's west shore. They stopped only to gather food for lunch and dinner on the sound, and then they unloaded the kayaks into the water.

The party consisted of one local, Steve, a Kill Devil Hills resident, who organized the trip, and four others, all from different parts of the country. Amanda and Andrew, siblings from Toronto, Grant, from Colorado, and Robert, from Virginia. Steve had a plan for some easy exploration, and then a stop for lunch. Finally they would do a nighttime paddle under the full moon that night.

It was a relatively easy paddle out to their first stop, Beacon Island.

Beacon Island was the remains of the old Civil War era fort at Ocracoke Inlet. Lunch was just an excuse to wander the island, which was just an excuse for Steve to tell his party the legend of Blackbeard, his death, and his ghost.

"You want to hear the story of Blackbeard?" he asked, knowing the answer before he said it. "The real story?"

The rest gathered around him in the sand, ready to hear a tale that they knew well, and discover so much more. Including something they would never expect or forget.

Steve began his tale...

"Blackbeard... did you know his real name was Edward Teach? Yeah? Well, that may have even been made up. He probably didn't want to embarrass his family. Anyway...

"Blackbeard was a pirate that sailed up and down the Atlantic and Caribbean, pretty good at it, too. He was famous enough to be feared, and even got a pardon from the governor of North Carolina, as long as he stopped being a pirate. Rich enough that he retired to Bath, a little town up the water from Ocracoke. But life on land didn't suit him. He got tired of his withdrawal from piracy, and decided he would go get a new ship. Well, that didn't sit too well with anyone who had a ship at sea, especially the governor of Virginia, Alexander Spotswood. He sent two ships inland to Bath to capture Blackbeard, only Blackbeard wasn't there. He had already left in his sloop, the *Adventure*. Unfortunately for Blackbeard, a lieutenant, Robert Maynard, was given command of two sloops, just in case Blackbeard headed to Ocracoke.

Which was just where Blackbeard was.

Maynard found Blackbeard, sitting high in these very shallow waters, just off Springer's Point. (Here the young narrator points to a far off beach, to the east and north.)

In the predawn darkness, Maynard rowed toward Blackbeard's sloop, no sails or flag flying. Blackbeard awoke to a mysterious set of boats moving his way. Blackbeard demanded to know who it was, and Maynard then raised his flag, signaling his intentions and threat. Blackbeard screamed out in the predawn gloom, 'Damn you villains, who are you?!'

Maynard responded, 'You can see we are no pirates!"

The pirate then screamed out, 'Damnation seize my soul if I give you quarters!'

And the battle was on.

Blackbeard let loose with his cannons, tearing apart one of Maynard's ships. Blackbeard then set his sails, planning to close in and cut the remaining ship to pieces.

What he didn't know was that in all the smoke and darkness, Maynard ordered his men below decks to hide and shelter from any attack. Only a few men remained above deck. The two ships both got stranded on the shallow sand bars all along here. The only thing they could do was to trade threats in the early morning light. Maynard fired his rifles into the rigging and disabled some of Blackbeard's sails. Both pirate and officer tried to lighten their ship to free themselves from the teeth of the sandbars that held them fast.

Once able to sail, Blackbeard closed on Maynard's sloop, the *Jane*. He threw grappling hooks over to pull the two ships close, and lobbed grenades, glass bottles filled with gunpowder and shot, over the deck. Blackbeard boarded the *Jane*, finding only a few men and Maynard at the bow. Blackbeard and his men charged at the huddle of Royal Navy seamen, boots slipping on a deck turned into a bloody abattoir from Blackbeard's cannon broadside.

At that moment, the forward hold burst open, with determined and well trained sailors charging into the now badly outnumbered pirates. What was a ship's deck became a slaughterhouse as the skilled sword fighters of the Royal Navy dealt death with the hungover pirates.

Separated into two groups, the pirates were quickly being undone. Blackbeard sought out Maynard, the commander of the opposing vessel. The two drew pistols and fired, their one shot each spent, and then brought forth their swords. Blackbeard's short cutlass was more than a match for Maynard's long sword, and the pirate cut the sword in half with one long stroke. Once disarmed, Maynard was under imminent threat by the bloody hand of the bloodthirsty pirate. His crew rallied to save him, surrounding the dreaded pirate, shooting and stabbing him until he fell, blood pouring from his many wounds, spilling across an already soaked deck, crimson with blood from sailor and pirate alike.

The rest of the pirates that survived the attack surrendered, and the battle was finally won. Maynard lost eight good men, while the pirate dead numbered four more.

In order to prove that he had killed the dreaded pirate, Maynard severed the head of Blackbeard and tied his long hair into a knot on a line in order to hang it from the bowsprit of his ship."

Steve paused his story, in order to make sure his audience was in rapt attention. "Now, here's a little part of the story that some people know, and others don't. Legend says that Blackbeard was still alive when he had his head cut off. Not just when it was cut off, but after," he stopped in mock gasp, the others smiling,

"History says that Blackbeard's head was removed from its body, hung from the front of the ship, and taken back to Virginia in order to collect a bounty. But legend says something else. Blackbeard's body was thrown over the side, left for the fish," Steve gestured to the water that surrounded them. "But he was still alive...

"His body wanted to join back with his head. See, the two wanted to be put back together so he could keep fighting. His body swam around the boat, trying to find his head. Imagine that!

"And the head, it was still alive! It was still early morning, and, supposedly, the head called out for the sun to rise so he could see better, saying, 'O' cry, cock!' Which was how Ocracoke got its name."

The other four sat in silence, at first. Then they burst out in giggles, delighted at all the blood and gore and legend.

"No way!" said Robert. "That can't be how the island got its name!"

"Nah," Steve laughed, "I was just fooling with ya. That's the legend, but the island has been called Ocracoke, or some form of it, since the natives were first here. But the rest of the stuff, the head being cut off, the body being dumped overboard, all that, it's true.

"They even say Springer's Point is haunted by Blackbeard's ghost. He's still searching for his head. It was said that he was so evil that heaven didn't want him and the devil was afraid of him, so he walks the beach, never able to leave."

"You think that's true?" asked Amanda.

"I dunno, but there's lots of spooky stuff that is said to happen on the island." Steve shrugged. "Skeletons walk the roads, ships on fire off the coast, hands that reach up from the grave, zombies washing up on shore, this place has it all.

"But you want to know something kinda spooky? Blackbeard's body was thrown overboard, right? But it never was found. And all the dead pirates? They were buried in an unmarked grave somewhere on the island. But no one knows where. And Blackbeard's ship was never found."

"So," Grant chimed in, "not only does Blackbeard walk around here, his crew could still be haunting this place, too?"

"Yes," Steve responded, "and tonight, we are going to find out if they walk the land. We're going out to Springer's Point for our moonlight paddle."

After a dinner in the village, the team of five set off at sunset with the moon already rising over the ocean, full and bright yellow. To their left as they paddled, tiny Ocracoke Light turned itself on, sending its beam over the water as a marker for the harbor at Silver Lake. It was no longer needed for shipping, but its light was a comfort, a touch of mankind in the dark of night. No matter where one was, the light could be seen, marking a way home. The sun boiled in the sound water to the west, and was extinguished as it sunk below the horizon.

The group paddled quietly, enjoying the still darkness, navigating by feel, following the darker shadow of the treeline, until they saw the white sand of the beach at Springer's Point, lit up by the moon into an eerie green. They paddled their kayaks up to the beach, grounding with a soft rush of sand on the keels.

"This is where Blackbeard's body is supposed to walk?" Robert said sarcastically.

"Don't mock!" teased Amanda. "He'll come for your head!"

"Blackbeard wouldn't want his head!" chided Grant.

"You just wait," warned Steve. "Listen…"

The five stopped talking, and the sounds of nature took over. Soon strange footsteps fell in the dark woods just next to them. The trees were only twenty feet away, but they were as dark as tar pitch. They gave away nothing to the visitors. Soon more footsteps were heard. Somewhere in the dark, strange animals prowled in the night, kept out of the light of the moon only by fear of the intruders standing in the sand.

"What does it look like?" whispered Amanda.

"What?"

"Blackbeard's ghost. What does it look like?"

"It's supposed to be a ball of light, floating over the beach."

Robert finally spoke up. "Aw, come on, we're not gonna see a ghost!"

Everyone could tell he was a little scared. The loud disclaimer was like whistling through the graveyard, a bluff to keep the ghouls at bay. The rest of the crowd was relishing the blood chilling silence, waiting for the ghosts to appear, but Robert was a little too scared. He began to move back to the kayaks.

The others sighed. The noises from the woods stopped. Whatever was out there had been silenced by the noise of the interlopers. Whatever magic there had been was now lost.

"C'mon," said Steve, "Let's go sail some."

The five people put their kayaks out into the water, now glowing with dim lights and glow sticks so they could easily see each other. The slow currents followed the deep pockets of water, the often changing channels that surrounded Ocracoke. Some water was deep, especially the boat channels for the sailboats and ferries that plied the waters, while other spots were shallow enough to walk, or strand a kayak. Some even formed tiny dry islands in the sound. The five of them found themselves chasing each other in the dark, occasionally stranding themselves only to run across a shallow sandbar to cast their kayak into the water on the other side. If anyone was watching, they would have seen five different lights dancing across the water as the little kayaks skipped across the sound.

"Hey," Grant asked breathlessly, as he had been running and paddling hard, "who's that?"

They all looked around, unable to see where Grant was looking. "To the south, guys. There's a light there. Who's got a yellow light?"

"It's not me," said Steve, shaking his bright green light. "Amanda's got red," she shook a long tangle of lights she wore as a necklace, "Andrew is orange, Robert's blue."

The five all looked around, seeing their own lights hanging from their boats. This was none of them. Steve turned on a small flashlight. He shown it over the water, but there was nothing there. When he pulled the light away, the strange yellow glow appeared again. It seemed like it was under the water.

"Let's go see," said Steve.

"Uh, c'mon, you guys, let's not get too near it, We don't know what it is." Robert had already been scared on land. Now surrounded by water, he had nowhere to go.

The rest turned together to go toward the light. But before a single paddle blade hit the water to move toward the light, the strange yellow glow began to move toward the five of them.

Separated from the others already, Robert began paddling frantically. He was already scared from being out on the dark beach, and now he was in the middle of the sound, away from the safety of land and lights, with a strange light coming after them from under the water.

The rest of the group were more fascinated than scared. The light almost flew under the water, avoiding all the kayaks, and heading straight toward Robert. He screamed, "Help me! It's after me!" And he was right. It zoomed up to him, creating a wave and wake, sending his boat pitching in the shallow water. Robert moved past frantic and into frenzy, splashing water more than pushing himself away from the terrorizing light.

Seeing their friend in trouble, and less afraid and more curious, the others took off after him. "Go to that sand bar!" yelled Steve, shining his light at a nearby scalp of sand.

Robert put his back into it, paddling deep until he hit the sandy bottom. He rushed toward the small island, beaching his kayak hard aground, and jumped out. He grabbed his boat to pull it firmly onto the dry sand.

The others watched as the strange light, gleaming yellow, circled lazily around the island. Every time Robert went to one side, pulling his kayak in the vain hope of escaping the underwater pursuer, the light would circle around to the same side. Robert ultimately ended standing forlorn in the middle of the island, with nowhere to go.

"What do I do? What is that?!" he almost cried in fear. "Why is it after me?"

The others hadn't noticed that before. They still sat in their kayaks, mere inches above the water, yet the strange light did not pursue them. Only Robert.

"I knew this was a bad idea! I told you we shouldn't have been on that beach!"

"What do you mean?" Amanda asked incredulously.

"It's Blackbeard! It's his ghost! He's after me!" Robert fairly shrieked the accusation.

The others stopped in mid strokes, all contemplating the accusation. There was no way it was Blackbeard, not a real ghost. Yet here they were pursued by an unearthly apparition swimming in the water, glowing under the calm sound. It was no fish, no animal, no freakish weather.

"You gotta help me! He'll take my head!" screamed Robert.

"Okay, stay calm, I'll come get you!" Steve tried to soothe his friend.

"NO! I can't leave the land!"

"Well... what do you want to do, wait there til he climbs up out of the water to get you?" Steve still didn't think it was a ghost, Blackbeard or some other ghoul, but it certainly was strange. Maybe...

"NO! We gotta get to land, get help. No!" he yelled as Grant began paddling to the village. "Don't leave me!"

"Well," said Grant, "How do you want us to get help if we can't go?"

"I don't know," Robert sad down, miserable, in fear and almost crying.

Steve spoke up. "Hey, go to one side, just enough to move it over there," he directed with his light. The strange glow circled around the island and away from the others in their kayaks.

"Now, let's go over here. It hasn't come near us. Put the boats in a line, two lines."

The four of them paddled to the near side of the little sandbar, pointing their boats outward, toward Silver Lake and the safety brought on by the beams of Ocracoke Light.

"Okay, quick, Robert, come out between us, right through here." Steve directed again with a light.

"C'mon, Robert," yelled Amanda. "We'll be around you!"

Hesitant, but terrified of being left alone in the dark, Robert at first didn't move. He looked at the glowing light, just offshore in the tiny waves that lapped the sandbar. He at least felt safe.

Then the light moved. It seemed to pull itself onto the sand. Robert's feet felt rooted to the island, his body unable to move. The light rose up, out of the water. It slowly took form, a waterlogged, disheveled shape of a man. Only without a head.

Arms reached out and up, heavy with water. As if it had only learned to walk, it took its first, trembling, unsure step.

Right toward Robert.

And, off in the darkness, somewhere in Springer's Point, came the call, "OOOOOOOHHHH!"

"Robert, NOW!" Steve commanded.

Spurred to life, and in fear of his own, Robert grasped the line to his kayak and began running, dragging the boat easily over the soft sand. He hit the water at a run, spraying his friends with the soft murky sound water. Still on his knees, he immediately began paddling. The others joined him, surrounding the young man with their boats.

Again a call came, "OOOOOOOOHHHHHH!"

Robert looked back, seeing the strange headless form reach up to the sky, but no sound came from him, only from far away. He redoubled his effort with intention.

The five kept up the strenuous paddle, not resting as they worked toward the boat ramps in Ocracoke Village. The town and lights seemed so far off.

Steve looked over his shoulder. The glowing man slipped down, onto the beach. Then he saw it. The light had moved back into the water. It began pursuing them.

"We gotta move, people!" he shouted.

Robert was already at the point of exhaustion, terror taking its toll, but he had the most to fear, and his back bent to the challenge ahead of him.

Closer and closer the group got to the harbor at Ocracoke, but closer still gained the glowing light, the strange headless ghost that chased one of them to an island just moments earlier. Steve saw that they were not going to make it, and turned his kayak sideways, into the path of the light. He splashed the water, hitting it with his paddle. The light got closer, but slowed just enough. Steve turned his kayak again, and paddled hard to catch up. The race was on.

Closer and closer the light got, and the kayakers struggled to get toward the lights of Ocracoke. They thought they would give out from exhaustion, and have to succumb to the whims of an aquatic spectral beast.

It seemed to take forever, but the group finally made it to the shore of Ocracoke Village. Four of them circled the waters while Robert jumped from his kayak and ran up the ramp. The others pulled themselves up and lifted their kayaks from the water. Tired past the point of movement, they looked out into the sound, seeing the light come closer and closer. Then, at the point of first touching the glow of the man-made lights of the town, it grew dim, faded, and disappeared.

The night passed quietly, having told only a few locals of their tale before being laughed off. No one was going to believe this story, they told each other. But they knew the truth.

The next morning, they loaded their kayaks into the two trucks they brought. Amanda shared her Jeep Cherokee with her brother and Steve, the three loading their kayaks onto the roof. Robert had driven his new Toyota pickup, shiny and black. One of the locals noticed the Canada plates on Amanda's Jeep, commenting on how far they had come on their trip. He then turned and admired Robert's Tacoma.

"Virginia, eh? Yeh know, Robert Maynard was from Virginia…"

He walked away from the group, down the road, laughing to himself, a baritone chuckle that echoed in the trees.

Afterword

As I said at the beginning of this book, you may recognize some of these stories as classics of Outer Banks lore. Others, while known to some locals, might be less well known. But all of them are certainly fun.

These are all stories I enjoyed as a kid and even now. When I was young, it was a rite of passage to read stories of the ghosts that were part of the Outer Banks. We all enjoyed pulling out the dusty books of Nancy Roberts or Charles Harry Whedbee. Both wrote wonderful collections of ghosts and legends along the coast. These were the books that gave us the heebee jeebees, chilled our blood, and sent us out to search for pirates on the wind.

I hope you have enjoyed the stories here, as I enjoyed telling them. Next time, we may gather at a campfire or sit by a pier as we tell our stories. We may have doubters, and maybe some true believers. I will say this, all the stories have some hint of a real history. Ghost stories are best when embellished, told aloud, a mix of whispers and shouts. These stories have the added benefit of being true, at least somewhat. I left off the reality of some of the tales in order to make it more fun.

I didn't want to spoil the magic.

Joe Sledge

About the Author

Joe Sledge is the author of four books of his Did You See That? Series on North Carolina's roadside oddities and hidden history. A longtime local of the Outer Banks, he spent every summer of his youth in an unairconditioned beach house sleeping on the sofa because everyone else in his family got the beds.

Joe graduated from UNC Chapel Hill and then was a special education teacher in California and North Carolina before writing his books. He now runs Gravity Well Books, his publishing company. When he is not writing Joe spends his time traveling with his wife and daughter.

www.ingramcontent.com/pod-product-compliance
Lightning Source LLC
Chambersburg PA
CBHW051025030426
42336CB00015B/2731